The
Snooze Alarm
Syndrome

THE
Snooze Alarm
Syndrome

When You Have the Desire,
But Lack the Discipline

Mary Whelchel

Scripture quotations are taken from the Holy Bible, New International Version.
© 1973, 1978, 1984 International Bible Society. Used by permission of
Zondervan Bible Publishers.

Cover design: Alan Furst, Minneapolis, Minnesota

99 00 01 02 10 9 8 7 6 5 4 3 2 1

Printed in the United States of America
ISBN 1-56955-168-5

Cataloging-in-Publication Data on file at the Library of Congress.
ISBN 1-56955-168-5

Dedication

To my "sister-in-love," Betty Stiles,
who is a true Superwoman. I can never
thank you enough for your loving care
of my parents during difficult days.

Contents

One

When You Have the Desire, But Lack the Discipline!

Turning Off the Snooze Alarm

I wonder what year it was that the snooze alarm feature was first invented. Seems to me it didn't happen before 1950 or 1960. At any rate, this modern device was welcomed by many of us as the solution to the problem of turning off the alarm and going back to sleep. The snooze alarm keeps bugging us to get up, going off every ten minutes or so.

It epitomizes the challenge most of us face on a daily basis— trying to put necessary disciplines into our lives so that we can be where we're supposed to be, do what we're supposed to do, accomplish what we need to accomplish and achieve what we want to achieve. We want to do the things we need to do, but it takes discipline and self-control, which come hard for most of us.

So at various levels we succeed or fail in our pursuits, in large part based on how successful we are at implementing "snooze alarms" into our daily lives. We have to find ways to quit procrastinating and make things happen.

If you are a naturally well-disciplined person, you need read no further. This book is not for you.

Some of us make it and some of us don't.

This book is for those of us who have failed over and over to make certain important daily disciplines a consistent part of our lives. It is for those who want to, who mean to, who try to, but often meet with failure.

If you are a naturally well-disciplined person, you need read no further. This book is not for you. That includes Betty (my sister-in-law) and Janet (my board member) and Dick (married to my best friend) and a few others I could name.

But for the rest of you, keep reading. You're like me—discipline is a major challenge and a lifelong struggle. It does not come naturally; it is not in your genes; you did not inherit it from your mother or father; and it takes a lot of effort for you to be a disciplined person.

Here's a quick self-test to determine whether you're naturally well-disciplined or not:

During the last thirty (30) days I have:

YES NO

☐ ☐ 1. Been late for work or some regular appointment more than three times.

☐ ☐ 2. Misplaced an important paper or document five times or more.

YES NO

☐ ☐ 3. Left a job unfinished three or more times.

☐ ☐ 4. Had to apologize for forgetting a meeting, date, appointment or commitment more than twice.

☐ ☐ 5. Been in a morning mad-dash at least five times.

☐ ☐ 6. Averaged less than fifteen minutes a day in a personal time of Bible reading and prayer.

☐ ☐ 7. Exercised less than twice per week.

☐ ☐ 8. Eaten fast food junk eight times or more.

☐ ☐ 9. Eaten fresh vegetables and fruit less than three times per week.

☐ ☐ 10. Missed an important work deadline more than once.

Here's how you score yourself:

1 or 2 "yes" answers . . . Your discipline is in good condition.
3 to 5 "yes" answers . . . Your discipline is in weak condition.
6 to 8 "yes" answers . . . Your discipline is in poor condition.
9 to 10 "yes" answers. . . . . . . Your discipline is nonexistent!

I thought of titling this book: *The Joy of Discipline*, or *Discipline Can Be Fun*, or *Discipline Made Easy* or *Delightful Discipline*. But none of those would do because I don't believe any of them. To me, discipline is a chore, a major chore, and if I could find some way to get through life without it, accomplishing what I want to accomplish, believe me, I would. Believe me, I've tried!

So why am I writing a book on discipline? Well, since the majority of the world is like me in this area (there are only a few naturally well-disciplined people), I figured that you wouldn't read a book written by a person who finds it easy and delightful to be disciplined. What do they know about those of us who are desperate, discouraged and, at times, defeated? How can they empathize with our plight? No sir, you need to hear it from one who has spent considerable time wallowing in the mud of intemperance and indulgence. One who still fights the good fight and sometimes loses. One who knows better than to tell you that discipline can be fun.

Discipline is not fun. But it is necessary. It's necessary, that is, if you truly want to accomplish something worthwhile in your life and reach your objectives. It's necessary if you want to turn your wishes into goals, your visions into realities, your dreams into accomplishments. It's necessary if you want to soar above the crowd and you're not willing to settle for mediocrity or mundaneness.

I find myself trapped in this human dilemma: I want to soar like eagles and blaze new trails and reach new heights. I have a driver personality to accomplish and achieve, but I am not a naturally disciplined person. Now, this can lead to a serious personality disorder (and some would contend that I have reached that point!). When you have the drive and desire but lack the discipline, you are one person going in two different directions, and that is terribly uncomfortable as well as unproductive! It leads to lots of self-incrimination and guilt and all sorts of other ugly emotions. It's a bummer; I've spent my share of time in that predicament, so I know what I'm talking about.

Discipline is not fun. But it is necessary.

Now, I suppose we can weed out a few other readers at this point by eliminating those who have no dreams, no visions, no desire to soar. If you're totally willing to live in mediocrity (or less) and there are no mountains you must climb or heights you must reach, you can drop out on me now, too.

However, before you close the covers, let me just make one very critical point:

Lack of discipline is self-inflicted suffering!

Did you get that? I would have written it in all caps, but I didn't want to yell at you. I do want you to hear it loud and clear, however, because if for no other reason, the truth of that statement may be the hook that keeps you plugging away on the road to a disciplined life.

Let me illustrate. Right this minute as I'm writing this sentence, the smell of baking pies is flooding my office. That's because we have a kitchen here, and one of my staff is baking pies for a luncheon at church in a couple of days. (Why do it on your own time when there's an oven at work?) More than anything, I want a piece of pie. In fact, she said if I'd let her bake the pies here, she'd bake an extra one for us. How could I refuse?

But this morning I stepped on my scale (and there are many days I'd like to throw mine at whoever invented them) and faced the fact that my weekend added two pounds (closer to three, actually, but if you take one foot off the scale, it helps!). I really didn't need to step on the scales; the button on my skirt gave me the same message, since it seems to be two inches tighter than before. So I reminded myself of my discipline for weight control: Never let my weight get more than two or three pounds out of line. Once it gets more than five pounds beyond my target weight, it's mission impossible to take it off. So I promised myself to lay off all the good stuff and eat the Lean Cuisine until the extra pounds are gone.

Wouldn't you know that today is pie-baking day at the office. And I'm faced with the choice of sticking to my discipline or indulging in the pie. Believe me, I could give you ten reasons why eating one piece of pie today would do me no harm. In fact, I could convince you that the best thing for me would be to eat that pie. I could wax eloquent on how much I deserve one little piece of pie. But I know myself better than that, and I know I'd never settle for one piece. I've always been of the school of thought that more is better, so having one tiny sliver of pie would never work for me. I know it does for some, but not for me.

This illustrates my point: Discipline is not fun! It's a truly painful and distasteful (excuse the pun) thing at times. But if I refuse to impose this discipline on myself, I will inflict suffering on myself. I will eat at least two pieces of pie, maybe more, and then I'll have to face the scale tomorrow morning, and the guilt and the realization that my goal to keep my weight under control, a few pounds at a time, is slipping away.

> When I start to lose discipline in one area of my life, it spills over to others.

I've also learned that when I start to lose discipline in one area of my life, it spills over to others. It's as though there's no need trying to be disciplined, since I blew it on the pie! So in addition to eating too much pie, I probably would skip the exercise routine in the morning, figuring, "What good does it do to exercise, when you ate all that pie yesterday?"

Now, I'm not saying that this is a rational way to think. It defies logic, I admit. But I am telling you that this is the way it works in this undisciplined person's life, and I know many of you are secretly saying to yourself right now, "Yeah, that's the way it is with me, too!" (And you thought you were the only one.)

You and I will pay the price for lack of discipline—every time. It is self-inflicted suffering. It has begun to dawn on me that, since I would not stand in front of a brick wall and continually bang my head on it because I don't like headaches, it is incredibly foolish for me to figuratively keep banging my head against the wall of lack of discipline. I suffer greatly when discipline is lax in my life, yet so often I continue to inflict that suffering on myself. That's just not smart, and I hate to think of myself as less than smart! It doesn't suit my self-image, if you know what I mean!

(By the way, I just checked the kitchen. They're chocolate chip pies. Wouldn't you know it!)

The Importance of Discipline

There's a whole book in the Bible written to teach us the importance of a disciplined life: "The proverbs of Solomon son of David, king of Israel: for attaining wisdom and discipline; for understanding words of insight; for acquiring a disciplined and prudent life, doing what is right and just and fair" (Prv 1:1-3).

Solomon is said to be the wisest man who ever lived. And I find his book of Proverbs, in the Old Testament, extremely practical for everyday living. In fact, because there are thirty-one chapters in Proverbs, I've developed the discipline (ahem!) of reading a chapter each day, corresponding to the day of the month. I would encourage you to do the same. Solomon wrote these proverbs down so that we could attain wisdom and discipline and acquire a disciplined and prudent life.

Now, right off that encourages me, because it says that discipline didn't come naturally for Solomon either. It had to be attained and acquired. Yippee! I'm not alone in the search for discipline. The wisest man who ever lived was in this same boat, and he has graciously recorded some very helpful information for each of us in our pursuit of discipline.

Here are some other choice tidbits that Solomon told us about discipline:

"Fools despise wisdom and discipline" (Prv 1:7).

"For these commands are a lamp, this teaching is a light, and the corrections of discipline are the way to life" (Prv 6:23).

"He who ignores discipline comes to poverty and shame,

but whoever heeds correction is honored" (Prv 13:18).

"He who ignores discipline despises himself, but whoever heeds correction gains understanding" (Prv 15:32).

Just to capsulize what Solomon said here, taking the negative approach, a person who refuses to be disciplined:

- is a fool.
- is poor and shameful.
- despises himself.

This is one time I'd like to think that the masculine pronouns limit these warnings to the male population. But I know my Bible too well for that; these "he" and "himself" references are gender neutral; they apply to us women as well.

But please, let's not overlook the positive message contained in these verses. A person who acquires a disciplined life:

- has chosen the road to life.
- has understanding.
- is honored.

To acquire a disciplined life, we will have to pay a price. But it's a big bargain.

Do you want to be more disciplined? Are you willing to acquire it? Join me, then, as I try to help you find some "snooze alarm" gimmicks, some ideas that may help you become more and more disciplined in your everyday life. I will be sharing from my own struggles and failures and—believe it or not—successes. I am living proof that anyone can acquire discipline!

And, for those who are "game," I will offer you a thirty-day challenge for each daily discipline, because I have found that most of us need a little impetus to get us started. That's the hard part, you know—getting started.

After thirty days of practicing a needed discipline, you will transition through the adjustment period. I'm sure you're aware that anything new we attempt to implement in our lives is, at first, burdensome and annoying, and it seems as though it slows us down or makes life more difficult. So, you need a thirty-day commitment to get past those first few miserable days and really be able to assess the benefits of the discipline.

Let me advise you that you should tackle no more than one or two thirty-day challenges at a time. If your enthusiasm overtakes you and you try too much at first, it will make success more difficult. So, choose the one or two disciplines most needed in your life, and work on those thirty-day challenges first. Then, when you make some headway in those areas, it will encourage you to tackle some others!

Remember, if I can do it, for sure you can, too!

Two

When You Hate to Get Out of Bed!

The Discipline of Getting Up Early

"I'm not a morning person!" How many times have you said that? It's one of the great clichés of our culture, and we have developed it into a one-sentence excuse that is seemingly acceptable justification for all sorts of usually unacceptable behavior. If I say "I'm not a morning person," then you must not expect me to:

- be at work early—or maybe even on time.
- take time for "morning devotions" or quiet time.
- look too good in the mornings.
- be energetic and enthusiastic before noon.
- be very productive before noon.
- be creative before noon.
- be polite and cordial early in the day.
- hold meaningful conversations until I've had three cups of coffee.

I ask you, do you know anyone who is a morning person?

After all, I'm not a morning person!

I wonder who invented that excuse. It has come to mean something akin to a disease, of which we are totally innocent victims. It's as though something in our genes causes this condition. "Aha," the doctor says, looking at the results of a blood test, "I see that your cholesterol is a little high, and you are a little anemic—and, oh my, you're not a morning person!"

But for those who don't want to get up early, this excuse is very handy. You're off the hook. No need for further explanations; no reason to feel guilty. You're not a morning person! And with such an incurable disease, you lower your expectations, cut yourself a great deal of slack and turn off that snooze alarm one more time, waiting until disaster is about to descend before putting a foot on the floor. After all, you're not a morning person!

I ask you, do you know anyone who is a morning person? A morning person would be described as someone:

- who bounds out of bed at the first buzz of the alarm.
- whose first words each day are: "Oh, good, it's time to get up!"
- who usually wakes up before the alarm goes off and shuts it off before it buzzes.
- who is cheerful right off the bat.
- who really detests staying in bed another minute or two, and just can't wait to start another day.

If you tell the truth, you are struggling to think of one person who is truly a "morning person." Most of us, left to our own undisciplined nature, would not be morning people. The morning people you know are those who, for the most part, have put that discipline into their lives. They don't have a special chemical combination in their systems that causes them to spring up at the appointed hour each day. No, they just get up early because it makes the day so much easier and more productive.

I can hear some of you thinking, "But Mary, there are some people who require more sleep than others. We don't all have the same metabolism." And I think that is likely to be true. I have to admit that my body doesn't seem to need a lot of sleep. I don't believe I need eight hours a night, not every night. There are others in my own family who have always slept more than I do.

Even as a teenager, I never could sleep until noon on Saturdays like my friends. And it was always so irritating to me that I couldn't call them before noon for fear I'd wake them up. I was ready for teenage chatter long before they opened their baby blues. Frankly, I used to be very jealous of those who could sleep until noon. I thought how cool it would be to have my mother tell my friends, "Oh, I'm sorry, Mary's not up yet," as the clock approached two in the afternoon on Saturday. I had great admiration for those who slept away half their days, when given the opportunity.

So of all the disciplines in this book, this one probably comes easiest for me, not because I'm a disciplined person, but because for some unknown reason, I just wake up early anyway. It is, I suppose, both a blessing and a curse.

However, that doesn't mean that I am a morning person. It just means I have some insomniac tendencies. I still struggle with getting up once I am awake. And I certainly don't "bound out of bed with great enthusiasm"; groans and moans are usually the first sounds out of my throat each morning, and coherent sentences do not come quickly or easily.

So Why Groan?

If getting up early is so hard, why not go with the flow? Why groan when you can get some more shut-eye? After all, there is no eleventh commandment saying, "Thou shalt get up before 6:00 A.M."

True, God didn't set a scriptural alarm clock, but the Bible warns about laziness and that temptation to replace work with a bed: "How long will you lie there, you sluggard? When will you get up from your sleep? A little sleep, a little slumber, a little folding of the hands to rest—and poverty will come on you like a bandit and scarcity like an armed man" (Prv 6:9-11).

OK, you probably aren't on the unemployment line because of sluggardness. But a lack of discipline can sneak up on us. "A little sleep" the Bible says; it doesn't take much. Before we know it, we're making excuses:

"No one will ever know if I get up fifteen minutes later."
"I just need a little nap."
"Later on would be a better time."

If we don't change our habits, poverty can sneak up on us too.

Proverbs offers the lazy another double-edged warning: "The sluggard craves and gets nothing, but the desires of the diligent are fully satisfied" (Prv 13:4). Would you rather have unfulfilled cravings or satisfaction? Is sleeping late worth losing out on full satisfaction? Diligence in getting up can have a host of benefits.

Why Get Up Early?

"Why is getting up early a necessary discipline?" you may ask. After all, it doesn't matter when you start, as long as you get it done. So one person begins at 6:00 A.M. and another 8:00 A.M. That just means that the early bird quits sooner. Right?

Most people who tell you they are not morning people will also tell you how late they stay up. Well, that's why they're not morning people. It's a "which came first, the chicken or the egg?" question. But here's the important question to ask about these late stayer-uppers: Are they accomplishing much in those late hours? Are they spending some quiet time with the Lord? Are they getting their minds prepared for the day ahead? Are they getting a head start on the next day's agenda?

If we monitored most of those "late-night people," I think we'd find that they are more often watching television or wasting time in some other fashion. Now, I know there are some who are productive until the last minute, but these are your naturally disciplined people for the most part. They are disciplined at every hour, and they are up early and late. It's not likely that any of them are reading this book!

Here are ten good reasons to get up early:

1. You'll get a lot more accomplished as an early riser.
2. You'll be in a better mood all day.
3. You'll be less stressed out because you didn't start your day in a hectic rush.
4. You'll be on time or—better still, early—at your job, and your boss will love you for that.
5. You'll have a leg-up on the competition.
6. Your mind has its most energy and creativity immediately after rest, so you'll have more good ideas and plans.
7. Your relationships will improve because you will have more patience to deal with people.
8. You can find some true quiet time in the morning hours, for meditating, communicating with God and becoming centered for the day ahead.
9. You can beat some of the traffic and avoid the worst of the traffic jams.
10. You'll look better because you'll have needed time for important grooming activities and clothes preparation!

What Is Early?

Let's face it—one person's early is another person's late. Who defines early, after all? Is there some magical hour that we all have to abide by, if we want to develop this discipline of getting up early?

No, it is not one size fits all. But you need to determine what "early" is for you. Here's the formula for doing that.

How long does it take you to shower, dress and perform all other necessary functions that make you look your best?

_____

How much time do you need to prepare and eat breakfast?

_____

How much time does your family require of you in the mornings? (Include such things as helping kids get ready for school, having needed time for communication with your mate, etc.)

_____

How much time do you think you should spend communicating with God through prayer and Bible reading each morning in order to be spiritually prepared to meet the day?

_____

How much time does it take you to get to work or wherever you must be for that first appointment or duty?

_____

How much time do you want to plan for the unexpected things that happen, to cut you enough slack so that you avoid most morning crises?

_____

How many minutes do you want to allow yourself from the time you hit the snooze button until your feet hit the floor?

_____

TOTAL   (A) ____ hours ____ minutes

What time is your first appointment, duty or responsibility? (What time are you required to be somewhere, like work?)

(B) _____

Count backwards from this time the total hours and minutes you have just calculated.   (C) _____

(B minus A = C)

There you have it: Your get-up-early time!

Here's an example, in case the logic of this formula seems complicated to you.

Example:

How long does it take you to shower, dress, etc.?

1 hour

How much time do you need to prepare and eat breakfast?

15 minutes

How much time does your family require of you?

15 minutes

How much time should you spend communicating with God?

30 minutes

How much time does it take you to get to work?

40 minutes

How much time do you want to plan for the unexpected?

10 minutes

How many minutes after the first alarm?

10 minutes

TOTAL   3 hours, 0 minutes

What time is your first appointment or responsibility?

8:30 A.M.

Count backward from this time the total hours and minutes
you have just calculated.   5:30 A.M.

See how easy it is? There it is—your get-up-early time. (For
those who are arithmetically challenged, you are allowed to get
someone to help you figure up your "early" time.)

Obviously, the less you have to do in the morning and the
faster you are at doing it, the later you can sleep. But please be
conservative in estimating your get-up-early time. If you think
you can shower and get dressed in fifteen minutes, for example,
then you need to decide if you're leaving home in the proper
attire, looking as good as possible!

Also, if you've only been spending five or ten minutes in
quiet time, I'm hoping that after reading chapter eight, you'll
want to increase that time considerably.

Ignore Your Feelings

At this point you need a plan of action to help you implement your new get-up-early time. What can you do to force yourself to do this? Remember, discipline is always a pain in the neck, so you're not going to like it. Please don't expect to like it. Please don't wait until you feel like getting up early.

Almost every morning of my life I must overcome what I call my "morning depression." Thankfully, I have never had serious problems with depression, and generally I tend to be in an up mood. But every morning I go into a "blue funk" upon waking, and the longer I stay in bed, the worse it gets. I am demotivated, sad, ready to quit, despondent, discouraged, negative—all of that and more.

I have learned that getting up early and immediately upon waking is my best weapon against this morning depression. It goes away ten minutes after I put my feet on the floor and start my day. But even though I know this from years of experience with myself, it still is a daily battle. Every day I have to reconvince myself that my world is not in total disarray, that God does still love me, that I am OK and I can overcome these horrible feelings of depression, and all I have to do is get up and get going. It has become a continual lesson to ignore my feelings and do what I know I need to do.

So, please, learn to ignore your feelings when it comes to getting up early. And learn to ignore your tendency to rationalize an excuse.

Here are our most common excuses for not getting up early:

- I got up early yesterday, so that lets me off the hook today.
- I had a hard day yesterday—or a late night last night—so I deserve to stay in bed longer.
- Five more minutes won't hurt!
- I don't feel good, so I need some extra rest.
- Nobody else is up, so why should I get up?
- I don't want to wake up others, so I'll stay in bed until someone else gets up.

Put a Plan in Place

One of the most important things to remember as you try to impose new disciplines in your life is that you begin with baby steps and build toward your goal. You'll read that in most every chapter of this book, because I believe it is a key to success for those of us who struggle with being disciplined.

If that new get-up time is earlier than you now get up—and it most likely is—then build up to that new wake-up time. Don't try to do it all on the first day. That's too big a shock to your system, and your body will go on strike when that alarm goes off on Day 1. You want to ensure that you have success at reaching your goals right from the beginning and gradually build up to your new and improved early get-up time.

Let's say that you realize you need to get up thirty minutes earlier than you now get up. Please, don't set the clock thirty minutes earlier tomorrow. That's too much too fast. Instead, tonight set your clock ten minutes earlier—at 6:50 instead of 7:00, for example. Make it your goal to get up at that time three days in a row. Then on Day 4 start getting up (another) five minutes earlier—at 6:45—for another three days. According to this formula, you will reach your new get-up time in fifteen days. That may be fifteen straight days or fifteen workdays, as you may be able to afford to have more sleep time on weekend days. But either way, you will have a plan in place that you can actually achieve! A little success under your belt will encourage you to continue until you reach your goal.

Here's the way you figure your start-up plan:

1. How many minutes earlier do you need to get up than you now get up? (A) _____

2. Divide that number by 3 (rounded off as needed).
   A ÷ 3 = (B) _____

3. Set your clock earlier by (B) _____ minutes for Days 1, 2 and 3.

4. If A is 30 minutes or less, add five minutes to B. If A is more than 30 minutes, add ten minutes to B.

$$B + 5 = (C)\ _____$$
$$B + 10 = (D)\ _____$$

Set your clock earlier by (C or D) _____ minutes for Days 4, 5 and 6.

5. Continue adding five or ten minutes to C or D in three-day increments until you reach your new get-up-early time.

"Snooze Alarm" Wake-up Gimmicks

Here are some practical tricks to play on yourself to help you get up early:

1. Put the alarm clock or radio out of arm's reach from your bed, so that you are forced to get up in order to turn it off.

2. Buy an alarm clock with the loudest, most obnoxious alarm you can find.

3. Ask your naturally disciplined friend (hopefully you have one), who is always up early, to call you early each day.

4. For every five minutes late that you get up, impose consequences on yourself. For example:
   - if you are five minutes late getting up, no jelly or jam on your toast.
   - if you are ten minutes late getting up, no toast.
   - if you are fifteen minutes late getting up, no cream or sugar in your coffee. If you don't take cream or sugar, buy a brand of coffee you don't like, and make yourself drink that coffee.

Write these incentives down and put them in the kitchen or wherever you will see them. Your list may be quite different from this one, because you know what will motivate you better than I do.

5. Make yourself accountable to someone whom you will see early in your day—your mate (though that may not be the best choice for marital bliss), a coworker or a friend. Give that person permission to ask you, "What time did you get up today?" Then, give a very honest reply with *no excuses!*

6. Start a chart or write on your daily calendar what time you get up each day.

7. When you have reached your desired get-up-early goal and stuck to it for seven straight days, reward yourself. Suggested rewards:
   • One day off for good behavior!
   • A special food treat that you don't normally allow yourself to have.
   • A long, relaxing bubble bath.

Try not to break your budget with your rewards, but rather choose rewards that are fairly cost free. Positive reinforcement is very motivating, even if you have to positively reinforce yourself!

The Rewards of Early Rising

The psalmist wrote: "Satisfy us in the morning with your unfailing love,

> Your day is won or lost in the morning hours.

that we may sing for joy and be glad all our days" (Ps 90:14). "I will sing of your strength, in the morning I will sing of your love; for you are my fortress, my refuge in times of trouble" (Ps 59:16).

Let me assure you that putting this discipline in place in your life is very rewarding. It will indeed give you the time to be focused on God's unfailing love, and that will make a huge difference in your attitude all day long. It will give you added strength for whatever troubles lie ahead for that day, known or unknown.

I have discovered that getting up early with a plan for those early minutes and hours to be used profitably truly affects all that I do. Your day is won or lost in the morning hours.

Here are some of the rewards of getting up early:

- It rids you of that cloud of guilt that hovers over your head when you know you started your day off the wrong way.
- It allows you to prepare for the day ahead, mentally, physically and spiritually, and therefore you will handle whatever happens that day far better.
- It motivates you to be productive and accomplish your goals for the day.

- It makes you a much better time manager, because you have some extra time to manage!
- It gives you a sense of being in control of your day, instead of your day being in control of you.

Take it from a person who still struggles with this discipline, but who has practiced it long enough to realize the benefits. This is one of the best gifts you'll ever give to yourself. If you will stop using the "I'm not a morning person" excuse and tell yourself, "I will learn to be a morning person," you have some great things to look forward to. Who knows—you may uncover skills and abilities that have been cooped up inside of you, and I promise, you will accomplish so much more than before.

Thirty-Day Challenge

Day 1:

Determine your new get-up time. Decide what gimmick you will use to get yourself up.

Days 2–15:

Start getting up earlier, working up to your goal.

Days 16–30:

Challenge yourself to get up at your new early time fifteen days straight without missing one day.

At the end of this thirty-day period, you will have the worst behind you, and you will already be enjoying the rewards of getting up early!

Three

When Everything You Like to Eat Is Bad for You!

THE DISCIPLINE OF EATING RIGHT

I really don't want to write this chapter. It brings on great feelings of hypocrisy, for this is one of the two most difficult daily disciplines for me personally. So for all of those who know me personally and interact with me regularly, please don't remind me of what I have written. Please don't preach my sermons to me when you see me breaking my rules. Cut me some slack! This one is tough.

First, let me put your mind at ease and assure you that I'm not writing a diet chapter, nor am I trying to pretend I'm a nutritionist. And I am most definitely not writing a chapter on staying thin! Most of us know a lot more about proper eating than we ever implement, so there's no need for me to add one word to the billions that have been written about what's good for you to eat and what isn't. You know enough right now without any further knowledge.

Let me illustrate this. List below everything you ate yesterday—or today if you're reading this after your three daily meals.

For breakfast I ate and drank:

_____   _____   _____

_____   _____   _____

For lunch I ate and drank:

_____   _____   _____

_____   _____   _____

For dinner I ate and drank:

_____   _____   _____

_____   _____   _____

In between meals I ate and drank:

_____   _____   _____

_____   _____   _____

- Circle everything on your list that is high in fat and cholesterol.
- Circle everything on your list that is high in sugar and calories.
- Circle everything that is fried.
- Circle every beverage that contains caffeine or alcohol.
- Underline every vegetable or fruit on your list.
- Underline every high-fiber food on your list.
- Underline every beverage that is good for you (skim milk, fruit juices, water, etc.).

See what I mean? You already know what you should and should not eat. You don't need more knowledge so much as you need to practice what you know. The circled foods are not so good for you; the underlined ones are much better. Do you have more circles than underlines? Was this a fairly typical eating day for you?

> Have you ever wondered why the foods that are bad for us are so tasty? It's one of my first questions for God when I get to heaven.

We all need to give thought to what we eat in a normal day.

Are Excuses What's Eating You?

It seems that every time we are told what is good for us to eat, not long afterward some scientific study done somewhere by somebody will seem to indicate just the opposite. One day eggs are no good for you; now they're backing off that strong stand against eggs. One day broccoli is the cure for cancer; the next day it causes some problem. So we all get rather cynical about this healthy diet, and we conveniently find excuses to eat what we want to eat.

Have you ever wondered why the foods that are bad for us are so tasty? It's one of my first questions for God when I get to heaven. Why can't brussels sprouts taste like chocolate? Why can't cottage cheese have the appeal of nachos? My mind keeps thinking how much easier it would be for us to eat right if the right things just tasted like the wrong things.

> **Temptation is the appeal of giving up the long-term good for the short-term pleasure.**

Sin has pleasures for a season. That can't be denied. Otherwise, we'd never be tempted. Temptation is, in reality, the appeal of giving up the long-term good for the short-term pleasure. Isn't that about the way it is? The temptation for sexual sin surely fits that description. It's also true for things like gossip—we actually enjoy gossip at the moment, so when we gossip, we choose short-term pleasure instead of long-term good.

So when I'm tempted to eat what is not good for me to eat, I want that short-term pleasure of the taste and good feeling that food provides, knowing full well that its long-term effects will not be good for me. But I have the most marvelous mechanisms for blocking out the long-term harm and rationalizing it away which I have carefully developed over years. Bet you do, too.

Here are some of the excuses we use to justify our bad eating habits:

- I'm in a rush and eating on the run, so I just have to take whatever is available fast.

- I travel a great deal, and it's very difficult to have a good diet when you have to eat out a lot.

- I eat a much better diet than _____. (Notice how we love comparison when it makes us look better, but resent comparison when it shows us up.)

- I have to shop and cook for my family, and they insist on all that bad food, so I have no choice.

- My kids/husband/roommate won't eat vegetables or fruit, so we never buy it.

- When I don't get three cups of strong coffee in the morning, I'm a miserable person all day!

- One of these days they'll prove that fried food is good for you; just wait and see!

- My grandfather ate anything he wanted; his diet was full of grease and pork and beef, and he lived to be ninety-five. I don't have to worry about what I eat because of my good genes.

- I'm not overweight, so I don't need to worry about what I eat.

I know there is ample proof that many people eat as a substitute—to meet some emotional need. For some it's loneliness, for some it's rejection, for others it may be a need to be loved or a longing for success. I'm sure there are those who eat out of spite and anger; life hasn't been fair to them so they have a right to eat what they want. I would not want to overlook those serious matters, and I'm sure that many who struggle with eating right need to take a look at how they are using food to try to meet these emotional needs. Food never does, no matter how much you eat.

But this book is not about those deeper issues. It's about our laziness and lack of discipline in forming good eating habits. I have often tried to search my own heart and mind to see if indeed I was trying to meet some emotional need through food.

> **Don't be too overly concerned about why you don't eat right; just put a plan in place to eat right.**

I suppose I may not know myself as well as I think I do, but I don't believe I eat for any emotional reason other than I like to eat. Food is good! I like good tastes! And since my personality always believes that "More is better," you can see where that gets me when it comes to food.

Whatever reason you have for not eating right, imposing discipline on yourself to force better eating habits will help you. So I would say, don't be too overly concerned about why you don't eat right; just put a plan in place to eat right. As Nike has taught us: "Just do it!" Without any scientific research to back me up, I would assert that most of us don't eat right because we don't want to deny ourselves that stuff we like so much!

Why Eat Right?

Eating right is not necessary *unless:*

- You want to live longer and better.
- You want to accomplish more in your lifetime.
- You want to feel better and look better.
- You want to be a good steward of your body.
- You want to avoid unnecessary disease and deterioration of your body.

So again we are not forced into this discipline of eating right. It is a choice we make.

Losing weight to improve your looks is basically a selfish reason for eating right.

I began to get serious about my eating habits as I watched my parents' health decline. My father's stroke and subsequent dementia has given me a clear picture of what could lie ahead for me, and I have recognized how much I've taken my good health for granted.

I've been blessed with extraordinarily good health all my life. Those of us in that category are very prone to abuse our bodies and overlook the need for good eating habits, simply because we're doing OK as it is! Formerly the only motivation I had for watching what I ate was to keep my weight down.

If that is your only motivation for eating right, it's going to be a long hill to climb. Think about it—just to lose weight so that your looks improve is a basically selfish reason for eating right. It leads to fad diets that are often harmful and to lots of up-and-down weight gains and losses.

I discovered that I could easily rationalize my weight when I wanted to, in order to justify bad eating habits. I would say to myself, "Well, I'm still in better shape than most people." Or, "I know how to wear the right clothes so you don't notice my weight gain."

If you are overweight, your focus needs to be on healthy eating, not eating to be thin. If you are not overweight, your focus needs to be on healthy eating, not eating because you are thin. The standards are the same for us all.

> We should get away from eating to look thin, and start focusing on how diet affects our lifestyle and our effectiveness for Jesus Christ.

Of course it's true that we all have different bodies and some of us gain weight much more easily than others. I can think of people I know—my daughter and son-in-law, for two—who have never had to worry about what they eat one minute of their lives. That's because they are both on the very thin side, and it doesn't seem to matter what they eat: They don't gain weight.

Of course, I have to admit that if I ate only what my daughter eats, I would probably lose weight, because her appetite is much less than mine. So what goes around comes around, I guess. But then again, I rationalize, "Why can't I have an appetite like hers? Why do I have to want the second piece of pie? Why do I always clean my plate and she doesn't?"

So I've spent more than my share of time in the "it's not fair" mind-set, excusing myself because somehow God just did not create us all equal, as our Constitution declares! If we were all equal, I would be as thin as Julie and not have to worry about what I eat. Frankly, that sounds like utopia to me.

Well, the facts are, I'm not like a thin person who can eat anything. I am a woman who can easily put on weight. However, my main concern should be not that I won't look so good, but that I won't feel so good. We should get away from eating to look thin, and start focusing on how diet affects our lifestyle and our effectiveness for Jesus Christ.

Eating Right Is a Spiritual Matter

It was only when I started looking at my eating habits from a spiritual perspective that I began to make some needed changes. The stewardship of my body started to take on new meaning.

In the parable of the talents, Jesus told us how three people were given certain talents and resources to use. These were not given in equal amounts: One received five talents, one two, and one received only one. But they were each held to the same performance standard, and that was to use what they were given to its best potential.

As you study that parable in Matthew 25:14-30, you will notice that the master rewarded the first two servants with equal rewards even though they did not have equal results. One multiplied five talents into ten; the other multiplied two talents into four. But to the master, that was equal performance, because they were both very good stewards of what had been entrusted to them to begin with. The last servant, with the one talent, did nothing, and he was strongly rebuked by the master because of his laziness and lack of discipline. "You wicked, lazy servant!" was what the master called him.

We often think of our "talents" as the money God has given us, but I would encourage you to think of it as the body God has given you. All of our bodies are different in shape, in metabolism, in energy levels, etc. But they are all given to us by God to be used as stewards. We are to take care of the bodies that we have so that we can multiply our gifts and be effective

> I don't want to stand before the Lord one day and hear about all he had for me to do that I didn't get done because I just didn't eat right.

for the Lord, and we can hear him say, "Well done, good and faithful servant!"

Ephesians 2:10 says: "For we are God's workmanship, created in Christ Jesus to do good works, which God prepared in advance for us to do." He created you and me for specific good works. Those good works are on his planning program somewhere. Before you were born, God had a plan for all he wants you to do. Since, as believers, we belong to him, not to ourselves, our desire should be to accomplish every one of those good works he planned for us to do.

What I eat is a strong determining factor in how much energy I have, how fast and long I can keep going, how creatively I can think, how long I live and, therefore, how many of my good works I will actually get done. I don't want to stand before the Lord one day and hear about all he had for me to do that I didn't get done because I just didn't eat right.

To fail to be a good steward of our bodily resources is to invite the Master's judgment on us. If I give out ten years earlier than I could have because of poor eating habits, I'm going to miss those ten years of service to God which he had planned for me. If I run at 75 percent of my potential because I don't eat right, I'm going to fail to do 25 percent of the good works God has planned for me to do.

For me, this is the motivating factor that spurs me on. And in spite of continuing failures, I am determined never to give up in my quest of eating healthy so that I can be a good steward of my bodily resources and stand before the Lord ready to hear him say, "Well done."

Starting Down the Road

There are many wonderful books available on good nutrition and eating habits. Some are even written from a biblical perspective. For example, *What the Bible Says About Healthy Living,* by Rex Russell, M.D. (Regal Books) is very helpful. So, I'm not going to attempt to duplicate any of that good work done by the experts.

However, if I'm right that most of us don't live up to what we already know, then I want to encourage you to begin to build good eating habits into your life. Again, start with baby steps and work your way up to it.

Find What Works for You

You need to discover what works for you. I'm convinced that there is no set formula that we can impose on everyone to create these good eating habits.

What I've learned about myself is that if it's near me, I will eat it. Since I'm single, I have the ability to keep food out of the house. My daughter and son-in-law have made fun of my refrigerator for years, and though I've lived in a new house for more than three years, I probably have used the oven only a dozen times. I don't cook just for myself. I microwave really well. But being single allows me to keep food away from me, and I know that is the only way I can keep from eating.

I know that indicates a weakness in my discipline and self-control, but I warned you from the beginning of this book that I am a struggler in this battle for discipline. So knowing my weakness, I try to stay out of temptation's way as much as possible.

I've also discovered a service where I can buy my week's meals all prepared, with a balanced diet, nutritionally sound and calorically minimized. I don't have to even think about what I'm going to eat. I just take the meals prepared for that day and eat them. When I can, I take advantage of this service, because it works for me. It not only keeps me from overeating, but I also feel much better when I stay on that balanced, nutritious diet.

I have found what works for me, and when I stick with it, I am able to impose this discipline on myself. So I want to encourage you to find what works for you and start implementing it. Here's how you do that:

1. *Start observing when you tend to eat too much.* Are there certain times of day that bring on a food binge? Do certain activities create an unexplained hunger? Do you eat too much at certain meals, while at others you don't eat at all or eat little?

For example, when I am writing, I tend to eat. Somehow through my years of being glued to computer screens because of writing deadlines, both for my radio program and my books, I have developed the idea that I can't write without food by my side. My rationalization is that I need that food to give me energy to be creative! I think it sounds very good, don't you? It's just not true.

2. *Start observing what bad foods you are most prone to eat.* Do the salty snacks get to you quickest, like potato chips, nachos and salsa, crackers? Or are you more susceptible to sweets, like cookies and candy? Maybe you're the hamburger addict, and you just can't pass up a Big Mac easily.

Unfortunately, I like all the bad foods. M&M's candy has never tasted good to me, but I can't think of any other junk food that I don't go for. What I wouldn't give for a distaste for these bad foods! If only they didn't taste so good and go down so easily.

When I'm driving a good distance, the golden arches are like magnets to my car. At no other time am I tempted with that fast-food junk, but I can smell McDonald's french fries fifty miles away, when I'm on a highway. It is so hard to drive by without getting just a small order of fries to munch on while I drive! My excuse for this is: I need to stay awake and the fries will help me stay alert! Oh, yeah? Who said? Well, that's what I say to myself when I want to justify the french fries.

3. *Start observing what you tend to eat too much of.* They may be good foods or bad foods, but you just don't know how to stop once you've started.

For most of us that includes peanuts and popcorn, but it doesn't usually stop there. I overeat bread! When the waiter brings the bread ahead of the entree in a restaurant, as they always do, I wolf down that delicious bread as if I've been on a starvation diet for weeks. Have you noticed that the bread in restaurants is almost always fresh, delicious and loaded with butter? Do you think there is some method in their madness, to get us filled up with bread before the real stuff comes along?

Again, I am inflicted with the "more is better" disease, and when it comes to the foods I like, that can be a disastrous way to eat.

OK, once you've analyzed those three questions, write down your answers.

I tend to eat at these times:

The bad foods that appeal to me most are:

I tend to overeat these foods:

With this simple analysis, you can easily formulate a plan for yourself to start working at eating better. Here are some suggestions:

1. *Clean out your cupboards and refrigerator.* Get rid of the foods that are really bad for you, especially the ones you are particularly attracted to. Give or throw them away.

2. *Stop buying the bad foods that you know you should not eat.* A friend recently told me that she continues to buy all the bad stuff she likes by telling herself that she shouldn't deprive her family of it just because she shouldn't eat it. But once it's in the house, she eats it, too. The truth is, as she admitted, that if it is not good for her, it is not good for her family either. So inform your family that there'll be some changes made in your grocery shopping, and they need to adjust or buy their own food. But it is not to be brought into the house.

3. *Replace the bad foods with good ones.* Instead of potato chips, try carrot sticks. They munch really well, and they're so good for you. Instead of french fries, have a baked potato without butter or sour cream. It's really good for you, especially if you eat the skin too. Instead of hamburgers, have turkey sandwiches, with nothing but lettuce and tomato on whole-grain buns. It will satisfy you, and all of that stuff is good for you. You get the idea!

4. *Limit how much you will eat.* One helping, no more. One piece of bread, no more. One cookie, no more. One piece of chicken, no more. Set explicit limits, especially on the things you love to overeat.

5. *Don't eat if you're not hungry.* When you're heading for a snack, ask the simple question: "Am I really hungry or am I eating out of habit?" That question has helped me greatly to stop before I get to the snack I'm heading for. Most of the time I'm not really hungry.

6. *Set time limits for eating.* For example, don't eat after 7:00 P.M. That will eliminate all those late-night snacks, which usually are very bad for us.

7. *Make yourself accountable.* One of my "sisters in Christ" in my Sunday Bible class at church has struggled with overeating most of her life. Now she has determined to change her eating habits and get rid of the sin of gluttony, as she calls it. Every Sunday she voluntarily reports to us how many days she has been free from gluttony. We applaud and encourage her. It is both a self-imposed accountability for her and an encouragement to her.

8. *Reward yourself occasionally.* When you've gone a week or so without breaking one of your good-eating principles, give yourself a little reward. Now, please don't overdo this. I'm talking one small piece of cake or pie, one small hamburger, some nachos. Whatever you really love but have been leaving off, because it's basically not good for you, give yourself a little reward by indulging—but this only comes after days and days of success at controlling your eating habits.

If any of you have come up with better ideas, I'd love to hear about them! I'm fully aware that this will be a fight until I die, but I refuse to admit defeat. So I'm open to your suggestions. We're in this together, and I know we can do it. I also know that this is one discipline which, when imposed, truly makes a wonderful difference in the quality of our lives.

Thirty-Day Challenge

Day 1: Clean out your cupboards and refrigerator. Go shopping for the right foods, focusing on breakfast first. Don't buy the bad things you know you should not eat.

Days 2–5: Work on breakfast. Determine what and how much you will eat, and stick to that breakfast commitment for five days.

Days 6–10: Work on lunch (while continuing your new breakfast menu). Shop if necessary for an improved lunch menu. Consider bringing your lunch to work instead of eating out. (It's much easier to eat right when you prepare it yourself than when you look at a restaurant menu and are tempted with all those things you should not eat!)

Days 11–15: Work on dinner (while continuing your new breakfast and lunch menus). Shop if necessary for better dinner menus, keeping them as light as possible. Eat before 7:00 P.M. if you can, and no snacks afterward.

Day 16: *IF* (big "IF") you have successfully accomplished all of the above, give yourself a reward and eat something you really want but shouldn't have today!

Days 17–29: Continue practicing your good meal eating habits, which are now fairly well established. Take a close look at your "snack" diet. Get rid of anything fried or fatty. For those who cook, be careful about snacking while cooking. (Mothers, don't eat the leftovers on the plates of your family at the end of meals!)

Day 30: Congratulations! You are well on your way to cultivating the discipline of healthy eating. Keep it up!

Four

When NordicTrack *is a Dirty Word!*

THE DISCIPLINE OF EXERCISE

My guess is that you may be ready to skip this chapter, and I don't blame you. For most of us, this is the most distasteful of all the disciplines covered in this book. And I can assure you that is true for me. I hate to exercise.

What Doesn't Work

Studies show that few Americans exercise adequately, in spite of the health clubs that have popped up on every corner and the exercise equipment that is for sale ad nauseam. Have you ever watched middle-of-the-night television, particularly those half-hour paid commercial programs? You will find endless offers of exercise equipment guaranteed to turn you into a gorgeous specimen of humanity in thirty days or less by using the latest and newest exercise vehicle. (Have you noticed that they all fold up easily and fit under your bed when not in use? I bet some of those babies have been sitting under beds for years, collecting dust!)

Well, I've tried my share of them. I've bought a bicycle exerciser, a NordicTrack and a rower. It just seemed to me that it would be so easy to use these each evening while watching the news, and each time I invested in those things, I was certain that I would use them religiously in that way. Never mind that I didn't use the last one; each time I was convinced that I would indeed use it and see the miracles in my own shape. Why, it wouldn't even take any time out of my schedule, since I watch the news every night anyway! What a good idea! I also strategized that by investing significant dollars into this equipment, I would have a sense of obligation to exercise. If nothing else would motivate me, money would!

Each has now found its way out of my basement storage area, either to a garage sale or into my son-in-law's basement as part of his exercise room. They never worked for me.

Beating the Boredom

I find exercise of any type extremely boring. Even speed walking on beautiful days is a chore for me because I'm always thinking about what I could be doing otherwise with that time.

Also, since I've been blessed with naturally good health, I never had a sense of urgency about the importance of exercising. After all, I was not a sedentary person; I was very active in my normal day, so surely this daily exercise program was not something essential for me.

Perhaps it would be helpful for you to check up on your exercise status. How much do you need the discipline of exercise?

TRUE FALSE

☐ ☐ 1. More than 50 percent of my working hours are spent in a sitting position.

☐ ☐ 2. I walk less than one mile each day, on average.

☐ ☐ 3. I cannot touch my toes from a standing position.

☐ ☐ 4. I get very winded when climbing one flight of stairs.

☐ ☐ 5. I avoid climbing stairs as much as possible.

☐ ☐ 6. I ache a lot after a little work in the yard, or doing something that requires physical exertion like stretching, bending, etc.

☐ ☐ 7. I can't do more than ten sit-ups at a time.

☐ ☐ 8. I have not used any kind of exercise equipment (machines, weights, stairs, etc.) in the last six months.

☐ ☐ 9. I get sleepy most every afternoon and have difficulty staying awake (the "afternoon dip").

☐ ☐ 10. I tire easily and my energy level is usually low.

If you have five or more "true" answers, you're not doing too well in this discipline. The more "true" answers you have, the more desperate is your need for an exercise routine and discipline.

If I had bothered to check up on my exercise status, I would have flunked this test. But with a strong body, I ignored my need for exercise.

Then I began to notice what I call my "afternoon dips." Between 1:00 and 2:00 each afternoon my energy would suddenly shut down, and for reasons unknown to me, I simply had no energy or stamina. I would have to take a break and waste an hour or so until that "afternoon dip" ended. This upset me because it interfered with my planned schedule and work effort for the day. Since I am such a controlling person, hating to have my schedule interrupted, I began to think about the causes of my "afternoon dip."

The deterioration of my parents' health also made me realize that my good or bad habits at this stage of my life will determine how well I age and how healthy I will be in twenty and thirty years. It really got my attention and made me face the fact that I had a responsibility to take care of the good health and body that God has given me.

As with eating right, I had enough general knowledge about exercising to know that everyone needs some kind of regular exercise. For optimal health, we need at least twenty minutes of aerobic exercise at least four times a week. (*Aerobic* simply means that you get your heart rate up to a certain level and keep it there in order to exercise your heart and keep it healthy.) I didn't have to read a book or go to a health club to gain that knowledge.

Furthermore, I knew that without exercising, losing weight or maintaining a desirable weight level was not possible. Good eating needs to be combined with exercise for the maximum health advantage. So I could not plead ignorance; all I could say was I hated exercise.

Finally, a few years ago, I made up my mind to find an exercise program that would work for me. If the exercise equipment was not the answer, what was? Well, I finally decided it had to meet these requirements:

1. *I had to be able to do it in my home early in the morning.* I was not going to pay big bucks to some health club and then have to be there on their schedule for classes or whatever. Since I do get up early, morning seemed best for me. I also realized that if I put it off until after work in the afternoon, I could find thousands of reasons to skip the exercise.

2. *I had to have something that gave me a sense of accountability.* For many people, this is exercising with a partner. I see my neighbors taking their power walks together in the morning. But again, I didn't want my schedule to be governed by anyone else's, so I didn't want an actual exercise partner, but something that would make me feel obligated in some way.

So again I played a trick on myself. I bought a step-exercise video and the exercise steps that came with it. I set up an old black-and-white television in my basement, bought a very cheap VCR, and began that aerobic step-exercise program five times a week for thirty-five minutes each day. This was not an expensive investment—around fifty dollars for the video and the steps. Having the video with the instructor there gave me that sense of obligation and accountability.

If you're wondering how I fooled myself in such a manner, again I cannot explain it. I didn't (and don't) dig into the recesses of my mind to figure out why it worked. If it works, that's all I ask.

For three years that has successfully gotten me into an exercise program. I have made it a part of the morning routine: Get up, make up the bed, put on the exercise shorts or sweats, grab a bottle of water and head to the basement. I am motivated by getting it over with. I get myself down there by thinking about how happy I'm going to be when it's over. I give myself kudos every time I manage to meet my video instructor and get through the thirty-five-minute program.

Frankly, there are days when I truly dislike the instructor on the video. I know her routine by heart, and I can't stand to hear her say the same thing every morning over and over. She never varies her routine. But I've come to gauge my progress by what she is saying. When I hear her say that same silly line again, I think, "You're one-third of the way through," or, "You only have ten minutes more." In spite of my antagonistic attitude toward the routine, however, she holds me accountable in some weird way.

It is also a daily competition for me to prove to her that I can get through it, all the way, no problem. Having a competitive nature comes in handy occasionally. I can't tell you how good it feels each time I finish to look her in the eye and say, "I did it, so there," and then turn her off and rewind her! It is a great sense of personal triumph.

> I try not to ask too many questions about myself, but just find something that works.

Sometimes on pretty summer days I will substitute a power walk for the video. When I'm out of town, I have walked hotel stairs for exercise, as well as taken power walks.

Lately, however, it has become more difficult to meet my basement instructor, and my routine has been seriously degraded. I think it was because I knew I had to write this chapter, and every discipline I'm writing about has become more difficult as the writing has commenced! (I'm going to choose my book topics more carefully from now on!)

Since my routine hasn't been up to its usual level of dependability, I've put off writing this chapter. What was wrong with me? It has worked for so long. Well, again, I try not to ask too many questions about myself, but just find something that works. It seemed to be time for a change.

So I have recently joined a club just for women. It is just one huge room in a shopping mall, filled with exercise equipment and a huge exercise floor. They have regular classes you can participate in, and their hours of operation start early and go late. For about $13 a month, I am now a "member" of this club. It is a few blocks from our office, so I'm stopping there in the afternoons on the way home, joining a class, using a couple of the machines, and finding this is working well for now. Again, it has an element of accountability, and having other women there doing the exercises with me increases my competitive drive. We'll see if this is a good substitute long-term, but so far it's working well. Eventually I may go back to my basement rendezvous with my video instructor.

Why Exercise?

Now, here's the reason I put myself through all this. The "afternoon dips" go away when I exercise regularly; the energy level goes up dramatically and very noticeably; I can work longer and more productively; I truly feel better; and I can manage some weight loss and maintenance when I combine exercise with good eating habits.

In addition, I find that I can think better when I exercise; because of the improved blood flow, my memory works better and I'm not so forgetful. And I'm certain that my heart has been strengthened through a regular exercise program.

Of course, like all women, I want to look young forever, and there's no doubt that regular exercise contributes to younger looks and a prettier figure. When I began to see the midlife flab on my arms, I said to myself that I was going to fight the signs of old age with all that was in me! There's nothing wrong with those motivations, either. We should want to look as good as we can for as long as we can.

But beyond all of these typical reasons for exercising, more than anything else I want to keep going to the end of my days, without debilitating sickness or physical handicaps. I don't have complete control of that, and God is still sovereign over my future. But it is my responsibility to be a good steward of my body. My body

> My body is a resource given to me by the Lord, and I am going to be held accountable for how I've used it.

is a resource given to me by the Lord, and I am going to be held accountable for how I've used it.

Paul wasn't afraid to get his body under control, when it influenced his ability to serve God. "No," he admitted, "I beat my body and make it my slave so that after I have preached to others, I myself will not be disqualified for the prize" (1 Cor 9:27). Paul wasn't vain; he wasn't even concerned with his looks. He wanted to be able to serve God with all his might. Like a boxer, discipline could help him reach his goal—service to God.

As I said in the last chapter on eating right, I don't want to miss out on what God has planned for me to do simply because I was too lazy and undisciplined to put a little exercise into my life. I don't want to live in such a shortsighted way that being comfortable for the present moment keeps me from doing what will make my life so much better in the future.

It would be hard to say which is more important: eating right or exercising regularly. They both go hand in hand. These are the two most important disciplines for our lives when it comes to our physical well-being, and our physical well-being affects every other part of our lives. We ignore them to our great harm and destruction.

What Works for You?

If you do not have some type of exercise program that you are regularly using, the purpose of this chapter is to encourage you to get one going. It won't be easy; you will probably hate it, as I do. I cannot tell you that it has gotten easier. I still hate exercise, but it's easier to motivate myself now because I have tasted the fruits of this discipline, and I know how much difference it makes in my life.

So your first task is to make up your mind that you will do it, regardless of how you feel. Since we live in a world that has taught us to be motivated by our feelings, it is more difficult for us to bypass our feelings and ignore their siren call.

Let me assure you that your feelings are not going to cooperate with you in your exercise program. Stop asking them to. You may never love it, or even like it. So, just be prepared for thirty minutes of unpleasantness at least four times a week. Lowering your expectations in this way helps a great deal.

There are some things you can do to reinforce your resolve to exercise. Choosing a routine that suits you is one important way. Analyze yourself and find what works best for you. Here are some helpful questions to get you going:

1. *What time of day am I most likely to be able to maintain a regimen of exercise discipline?* What time of day do I have the most control over my schedule, where I am least likely to have interference from other commitments or responsibilities?

- Mornings would be best for me, since my afternoons and evenings are very unpredictable and variable.

> I still hate exercise, but it's easier to motivate myself now because I have tasted the fruits of this discipline.

- Midday is my best time, since I can take a needed break and pick myself up thereby. I almost always have an hour or so at midday over which I have control.

- Afternoons are best, after my work is completed but before the evening routine begins.

- Evenings would work best for me. I have more discretionary time then. Besides, I'm not a morning person!

- I would need a variety of times for my exercise, depending on the day of the week. Morning would work best for weekdays but afternoons would work best for weekends (or vice versa).

It's most important that you set the right time up from the beginning. If you choose the wrong time, it will just give you one more excuse to bail out before you really get this discipline established. So, carefully consider what time is best for you.

2. *What type of exercise program am I most likely to stick with?*

- I need something that I can do by myself on my own schedule.

- I need to exercise with other people. It won't work for me if I have to do it alone.

_ I prefer exercise out of doors, enjoying God's beautiful nature.

_ I prefer exercise indoors to avoid weather or daylight problems.

_ I prefer something simple that does not require equipment of any kind.

_ I prefer using equipment where I have more control of the speed, time and level of advancement.

_ I would be more serious about exercising if I joined some type of club (and I can afford to do that without causing financial difficulties).

_ I am very competitive by nature, so I prefer a type of exercise where I can compete—such as running or tennis or handball.

_ I need accountability and progress reports.

Think carefully about your methodology. Hopefully you've had enough experience and attempts in the past at exercising (and some failures!), that you have a good idea of what works best for you. If not, you will need to use the old trial-and-error approach until you find your best method.

Try to avoid big investments of any type until you are certain it will work for you. Take it from one who has wasted money on exercise equipment: You can exercise without spending a penny. Investing money is no guarantee that it will work for you. If you're thinking that some type of club would be best for you, try it out before joining. They will give you guest passes to try to entice you, so use that as a way to see how it works for you. If you think a video might be a good idea, try one of the television workout programs for a few days to see if you can truly relate to a video instructor.

Again, start simple with something that you can do easily. Take baby steps; don't dive in over your head and become discouraged before you really get this discipline going. If exercise is totally a new thing for you, start with fifteen-minute walks for a week. Ease yourself into it. That's important mentally and physically.

Thirty-Day Challenge

Choose four days each week for a workout of at least thirty minutes. That's a total of two hours per week. Just 2 hours out of the 168 hours in each week—that's 1.2 percent of your weekly time. That's not asking a lot, is it?

These first thirty days will be a struggle, but every day just tell yourself, "It's only for thirty days, and I only have _____ more days to go." You definitely can see light at the end of that thirty-day tunnel.

After thirty days, assess the benefits of your exercise program. If you cannot identify visible, recognizable benefits from your exercise, then quit it. Fair enough?

But you see, I have no doubt that if you truly exercise for two hours per week in some type of aerobic exercise of thirty minutes each, you will quickly start to notice the difference it makes in you and for you. And you will be convinced that you must keep it up. In fact, you will want to increase it and enhance it.

My Thirty-Day, Thirty-Minute Plan

For thirty (30) days, I plan to exercise on the following four days each week:

- ☐ Mondays
- ☐ Tuesdays
- ☐ Wednesdays
- ☐ Thursdays
- ☐ Fridays
- ☐ Saturdays
- ☐ Sundays

Each of these four days I will exercise for at least thirty (30) minutes doing the following:

- ☐ Floor exercises
- ☐ Walking
- ☐ Running/jogging
- ☐ Step aerobics
- ☐ Exercise classes
- ☐ Using exercise equipment
- ☐ Using exercise videos

This plan will begin on _____ (date)
and continue until _____ (30 days later).

At the end of this thirty-day trial period, I will assess the results, and if there are positive differences in my life, I will, by God's grace, continue to make exercise a part of my daily life, and I will continue to impose this discipline so that I can be all that God wants me to be, for his glory.

Signed

_____

Remember, it's only a thirty-day trial period.
You can do it!

Five

When Being on Time Is Tough!

THE DISCIPLINE OF GOOD WORK HABITS

We no longer wonder what's happening when someone's wrist alarm goes off in the middle of a meeting or a church service or a concert or next to us on an airplane. "Oh," we think, "his or her alarm went off." It hardly seems rude any longer. Just another sound of the times.

That's what this new age of electronics has done for us. From alarm clocks with snooze alarms to alarm watches, we have lots of indications that many of us have a need for gimmicks and help in order to remember to do what we're supposed to do. Therefore, it would stand to reason that as a whole, we have better work habits than before, because we have more ways to prod and pull ourselves. Right?

I doubt if that is true. My experience, especially in the workplace, is that good work habits are fewer and farther between than a few years ago. Fewer people are on time; not many return phone calls promptly; follow-up seems rare; details are

> Good work habits will go a long way toward making you and your organization successful.

falling through more cracks. The little things that come under the heading of good work habits have become so rare that when someone demonstrates them, we notice as though that person were extraordinary.

The wonderful company that published this book, Servant Publications, has been a joy for me and my staff to get to know. Everyone we have met and worked with in that organization has been not only friendly and encouraging, but dependable and trustworthy. They return phone calls; they follow up; they remember to do what they promise. My staff and I remark about it frequently and talk about the pleasure it is to work with these folks.

Funny thing is, they seem to feel the same way about us. Many times they have commented that it's not difficult to get through to us, and we are prompt in fulfilling our commitments, etc. I guess we have a bit of a mutual-admiration society going here, but the reason is, we've both had so many bad experiences with people and companies who simply do not have good work habits.

Good work habits will go a long way toward making you and your organization successful. You may not be the smartest person on the block, you may not be the fastest worker, you may not have the most talent or experience, you may not have as high a level of education as others around you. But there is one way in which you can excel, regardless of these things. You can have good work habits if you want to. And believe me, good work habits will win out over talent or IQ or education or experience or speed alone every time.

You can have good work habits if you want to.

So in this chapter I want to talk about a few of the most common and most helpful work habits and suggest some ways you can put a "snooze alarm" in place to help you develop and maintain these habits.

A Noble Example

With all the things we have to accomplish in a day, it's not hard to make excuses for being late and having poor work habits. "Well," we might object, "people in biblical times didn't have such a busy world. They didn't have computers, e-mail and places to go. It was a different world, and God can't hold us to their standards."

We'd be dead wrong. Consider that people in biblical eras didn't have washing machines, cars and all the labor-saving equipment we have. Yet at least one woman accomplished even more than many of us do in a day. Turn to Proverbs 31 and meet the wife of noble character.

You don't have to be a wife to appreciate all the tasks this woman accomplished. Married or single, you can relate to all the things that filled her day: getting up at dawn to get things in order in the household (v. 15), household chores (v. 13), food shopping (v. 14), financial investments (v. 18), making thread for cloth (v. 19). Whether you do similar tasks for a family or just yourself, they have to get done. It's a busy schedule, today or hundreds of years ago.

Few of us can plead that we are more busy than the woman of Proverbs 31, who didn't have a car to do her shopping or a refrigerator in which to store food for days. On top of that, she couldn't order clothes through a catalog or go to the store and pick them up. She had to weave the entire family's clothing or have someone else weave them.

Yet her household ran smoothly while she planted a vineyard and took part in trade (vv. 16, 18, 21, 27), and she was never idle. Because of this, her husband and children called her blessed—not late or inefficient. People could see that it was God she served, not just her family (v. 30). She did things well, with an eye to the needs of her household.

If we want people to recognize our faith and value us as workers, we need to have the kind of work habits the Proverbs 31 woman showed. Obviously she had discipline, an ability to be on time and expertise at organizing her life. A few disciplines can make each of us into people whose "works bring ... praise at the city gate" (v. 31).

Being on Time

We might as well start at the beginning, and that is the good work habit of being on time. If we interviewed people who know you well, would they describe you as a person who is always on time? When I think of people in my life, several names pop right up to the surface as on-timers: LaVerne and Bertie and Phyllis and Heather and Michael and Robin. I'm sure there are some others, if I

Being an on-time person distinguishes you quickly.

scratched my head a little more, but my point is that being an on-time person distinguishes you quickly.

What makes these people on-timers? My guess is that first of all, their parents taught them to be on time and role modeled it for them. Not only were we on time as a family, but I remember that we were almost always early. My father and mother thought it was a shame to be late, especially to church. The idea passed on to us was that good families were on-time families.

Now I realize that failing to be on time is not the most serious character defect; I'm just pointing out that when you teach a child this good habit from early days, it usually sticks. My good friend Fran decided to try to help her Sunday Bible class learn this good habit of being on time. She noticed how many of them were showing up more than fifteen minutes late for church. She kept encouraging them to try to be on time, but words didn't seem to make an impact. So she began putting a sign on the class door each Sunday at fifteen minutes past the start time. The sign says, "Sorry. See you next Sunday!"

Now, I'm not necessarily recommending this for every situation, because Fran has a unique personality that allows her to do things like that in love and get by with them. But instead of resenting it, the class is making an effort to get to church on time, and guess what, it's working. At a recent morning meet-

---

Getting up early doesn't guarantee that you will be an on-timer.

---

ing of the class leadership, Fran noticed that everyone was not only on time; they were early.

What Makes People Late?

Why are people habitually late? Here are some of the reasons:

- *They don't start early enough.* The discipline of getting up early is not in place, and so every day begins with a mad dash and a late arrival.

- *They don't set a "drop dead" time to leave.* This will allow them enough time to arrive on time. Every day I have a "drop dead" leave-home time in my mind, which I either establish the night before or as soon as I get up. I assess my day, determine when I need to be where I'm headed and calculate what time I must leave the house. Then I manage my morning around that "drop dead" time.

    When you don't have this kind of mental discipline, even if you get up early enough you can squander away your time and lose track of it, and still end up being late. So, getting up early doesn't guarantee that you will be an on-timer.

- *They don't allow for Murphy in their "drop dead" time.* You know Murphy, I'm sure. That little gremlin who promises, "If anything can go wrong, it will." If you don't put Murphy in your schedule, you'll find that often you are late because "something went wrong." The traffic was worse than usual; you had to warm up your car; you had to wait for a long freight train to pass; all the lights were red that day—and on and on.

- *They try to do too much in too little time.* This is my greatest struggle in this area. If I am late, it will be because I was too ambitious about what I thought I could accomplish before my "drop dead" time and find myself scurrying to get somewhere on time. I plan a certain agenda before departing and my competitiveness drives me to try to accomplish it even though there is not enough time. I compete with the clock. It's as though I have a personal vendetta to prove to that clock that I am Superwoman, and I can get all this done before it's time to go. Well, I hate to admit it, but my Superwoman cape is pretty droopy. And sometimes this pursuit of Superwoman causes me to be late.

  I remember trying to get to a radio studio in Chicago one day for a live one-hour call-in program, "Mid Day Connection," where I am often asked to be a guest. I had a lot to do that morning, so I cut it too close and found myself embroiled in famous Eisenhower Expressway traffic here in Chicago. I got on my cell phone and tried to answer listener questions while driving in the rain, through

> To be a habitually late person is to show disrespect for others

tunnels, with lots of traffic. It was not a pretty scene. I finally arrived at the studio about fifteen minutes late, and listeners all over America knew that I was not an on-time person! Embarrassing. And all because I just had to get one more thing done before I left, combined with my failure to allow for Murphy time.

- *They don't have enough respect for others.* Most often when people are late, they inconvenience someone else. How many meetings have you been in where the first ten or fifteen minutes was wasted waiting for some latecomers? How many times have you had to do someone else's job because he or she was late? To be a habitually late person is to show disrespect for others; there's no other way to put it. It is a lack of consideration of their time.

- *They want to appear more important, more busy, more occupied than others.* They think that being late gives that impression.

- *They just lollygag!* They simply don't think about hurrying. It is not a concept with which their personalities are familiar. Life is to be lived; roses are to be smelled; people are to be talked to; ideas are to be explored. Clocks? Please, don't let clocks get in the way of enjoying life!

Analyze your own reputation for punctuality.

CHECK ONE

☐ I have a reputation for always being on time. I am almost never late for work or other events, and when I am, there is an extremely good and justifiable reason.

☐ I have a reputation for being on time most of the time (meaning at least 85 percent of the time).

☐ I have a reputation for being late a lot (50 to 85 percent of the time).

☐ I have a reputation for always being late. I am almost never on time, and in fact, people generally give me earlier times to trick me into being on time!

If you honestly analyzed yourself as always being on time, this is one discipline you've nailed, and good for you! It's a very important work habit that is often overlooked.

But for those who struggle with being punctual, which of these reasons is your most common reason or excuse for being late?

CHECK ONES THAT APPLY:

☐ I just don't get up early enough. (The ideas in chapter two will solve this problem.)

☐ I hate to be the first person to arrive. It is uncomfortable.

☐ My family and role models were never on time for anything, so I've just developed a bad habit.

☐ It seems that the people who are late are the ones who are most important; have the most to do. That's how I see myself.

☐ I try to get too much done in short time frames, and that causes me to be late.

☐ I fritter away my time, and then realize I'm in a time crunch!

☐ I always intend to be on time, but I never seem to leave enough time to get there!

☐ I'm just a laid-back person. It's not my personality to be prompt.

Seriously analyze the causes of your tardiness. Then think about the problems it causes. For example, how many reprimands have you received at work, school or church because of being late? How many people get irritated with you on a regular basis because you're always late? How has your tardiness affected your relationships? Do you think it has affected your career adversely? What crises are created because of your habitual tardiness? How much stress do you inflict upon yourself because of last-minute rushing?

I'm convinced we perpetuate most of the stress in our lives by our lack of discipline, and this is one of those examples of unnecessary stress caused by tardiness.

What can you do to impose this discipline in your life? I think of my niece, Susan. She and her husband, Danny, have four wonderful children, and like all children, they're all different, with their own personality strengths and weaknesses.

When her youngest daughter, Allie, was getting toward kindergarten age, she noticed that Allie was always late in getting ready to leave each morning. This caused family stress, because

> We perpetuate most of the stress in our lives by our lack of discipline.

she caused everyone else to be late. Her tardiness is a result of her laid-back personality. She simply gets so involved with what she's doing at the moment—like playing with dolls—that she forgets she has to hurry up and get ready to go.

So Susan gave her a choice. She could either get up with the rest of the family and stop wasting time so she could be on time, or she could get her up earlier so that she could take her time and dilly-dally as she pleased, but still be on time. It turned out that Susan had to start waking her up earlier than the other three, so she would not keep the rest of the family waiting. Allie wasn't thrilled about it, but she learned an important lesson. Being on time is important, so you'll have to impose some discipline on yourself to make sure you are on time.

Suggested "Snooze Alarm" Gimmicks

Here are some ideas to help you establish this good work habit in your life and be on time all the time:

1. *If oversleeping is your problem,* refer to the gimmicks in chapter two on getting up early.
2. *If you lose track of time too often,* set your clocks ahead by fifteen or twenty minutes. Again, you are playing tricks on

> Good work habits will go a long way toward making you and your organization successful.

yourself, but I can assure you it helps. My sister-in-law, who is naturally disciplined, has all the clocks in her house ahead. We all know they're ahead, but it still sends a message: Be on time. My clock in my car is consistently five minutes ahead. You'd be surprised how that helps me be punctual.

3. *Set a "drop dead" time every day,* at the beginning of the day and for other appointments throughout the day.

   Once you figure your "drop dead" time, add 20 percent for Murphy. For example, if it should take you thirty minutes to drive to an appointment, set your "drop dead" time thirty-six minutes ahead. Also, in figuring your departure time, allow for door-to-door time, not just drive time. It takes time to get into and out of the car, as well as walk to the door.

4. *Allow extra time for unusual conditions,* like bad weather. One drop of rain on a Chicago highway increases your drive time by five minutes. One flake of snow hikes it up by at least ten. Mondays are worse than any other day. All of these external conditions have to be considered in advance if you are going to be an on-time person.

5. *If you think being the last to arrive is important to your image,* it's time to change your thinking. Think about establishing a strong reputation for being punctual. Think about how surprised everyone will be when they discover that you've changed and are now punctual. You'll be far less stressed and embarrassed, not to have to explain why you're late all the time.

I use self-talk daily to impose discipline in my life.

6. *If you try to squeeze too much into too little time,* train yourself to stop early. I have to continually relearn to be conservative in estimating how much I can accomplish before time to leave. I've learned to talk to myself in these situations. I say things like, "Mary, if you get started on this, you're going to be late." "There's nothing that says you have to get all this done before you leave. It's your own artificial requirement, so let it go." "If you're late, you set a bad example for others." "You can't expect of others what you don't practice yourself."

Have I mentioned how important it is to talk to yourself? That includes inside your head and out loud. (You just need to exercise judgment about where and when you do this self-talk out loud, because some might find it strange.) Quite frankly, I use self-talk daily to impose discipline in my life. And I say some of the same things to myself over and over, but it works as a way to remind me that this discipline is necessary and important. In effect, I become my own cheerleader or my own disciplinarian or my own encourager.

Remember that being late is inconsiderate of others and does not show a Christ-like thoughtfulness of their time. So pray for an attitude of selflessness that will help you put the concerns of others ahead of your own and be on time for their sake.

Returning Phone Calls Promptly

With answering machines and voice mail, it is rare these days to talk to a real person. Aren't you surprised when someone answers the phone in person? We've all become addicted to these electronic message takers and in fact, they can be very useful in avoiding phone tag and multiple messages.

However, the old-fashioned habit of returning phone calls promptly has not been replaced by these machines. It is still an important element in establishing professionalism, attention to detail, dependability and consideration.

My stint as a saleswoman with IBM imbedded this good habit in me, and I'm grateful for that. I was told in no uncertain terms that my calls had to be returned within certain time limits. Managers checked on us to make sure we were taking care of those messages. To allow a phone message to go unanswered for more than a couple of hours was high treason in IBM. (And this was before voice mail and beepers and car phones.) Could that habit have something to do with that company's success?

Perhaps you've gotten into some bad habits in this area, and you simply need to remind yourself that this is important. Here's what you can do to help you replace the bad habit with a good one:

- Set a time limit for returning calls. Determine that you are going to try to return calls within an hour. Challenge yourself to do it.

- Check your voice mail or message machines frequently, especially on the job. Don't allow those electronic conveniences to become crutches and enablers of bad habits.
- Don't put off the calls you don't want to make. Do them first, and get them behind you. It makes the others seem easy.

If you've been lax about returning phone calls, I challenge you to change that bad habit for one week. Just give it a try, and make a real effort to return your calls very promptly. Then get prepared for the reactions you are going to receive on the other end of that phone.

You're going to be amazed at the number of times you'll hear a pleased voice saying, "Oh, Judy, it's you. Wow, that was fast." Or, "Oh, Jim, I wasn't expecting to hear from you so quickly." Or "Whoa, Ann, this is some kind of record—I just called you half an hour ago. Thanks for returning my call."

I guarantee that you will hear many responses like this from people who are surprised, but very pleased, to hear your voice in such a prompt reply. It's one of the easiest ways to build trust in a business relationship. Returning phone calls promptly sends a very good message about you, and it's not that hard to do. It just takes a little—you know—the D word!

Keeping Promises and Commitments

"Underpromise and overdeliver" is a good motto to remember. When was the last time someone made a commitment or promise to you and failed to keep it? How did that affect the

> ## Anytime you make a promise or a commitment to someone, you build hope in that person.

way you feel toward this person?

Proverbs 13:12 says, "Hope deferred makes the heart sick, but a longing fulfilled is a tree of life." Anytime you make a promise or a commitment to someone, you build hope in that person. He or she is hopeful that you will do what you've said you would do. If you fail to keep that promise without a good reason or explanation, then it does something to that person's heart—to his or her feelings toward you.

The person to whom you broke your promise is disappointed, of course, and may feel betrayed because you didn't remember or care enough to keep your promise. It's a form of rejection, when you think about it. Obviously that doesn't have to happen very often in a relationship before it takes a terrible toll.

Solomon, the wisest man who ever lived, tells us, "It is better not to vow than to make a vow and not fulfill it" (Eccl 5:5). Promise keeping is a very important work habit.

Which of these would best describe you?

CHECK ONE:

☐ My friends, family and coworkers consider me to be very dependable.

☐ I am dependable most of the time.

☐ I make promises too easily, usually feeling pressured to do so, and then often end up breaking those promises or commitments.

If you have to admit that dependability is not one of your strong suits, I encourage you to dig deeper and ask yourself why you have developed this bad habit of being undependable, of breaking promises. It could be lack of good role models in your life, laziness, self-centeredness, a lack of organization and a tendency to forget or many other things.

> Procrastinators tend to say things like: "I do my best work under pressure." Or, "I just have trouble getting started."

Whatever has caused you to be this way, it's time to take responsibility for your behavior and start doing what you need to do in order to become a very dependable person.

Not Putting Things Off

"Do it now and do it right!" Often those words just seem to scream in my ears. That's because I can fall into the bad habit of putting things off—at least the things I don't really want to do!

Are you a procrastinator? Procrastinators tend to say things like: "I do my best work under pressure." Or, "I just have trouble getting started." We can find all kinds of excuses for procrastinating, but if we face the music, we'll have to admit that procrastination creates many problems for us. Here are some of the reasons we procrastinate; see if you can identify with any of them:

- We procrastinate because we're simply lazy.
- We put things off when we're facing an unpleasant task or something we just don't enjoy doing.
- We procrastinate when the task seems overwhelming—too big.
- We procrastinate when we feel insecure about how to do it or we're afraid of failing.
- Often we procrastinate because we don't know how to get started.

Procrastination can become a deadly bad habit, and if you struggle with this, I want to strongly encourage you to make this a matter of serious prayer and determine how you're going to break the bad habit. First, identify where you tend to procrastinate the most and ask yourself why. God says he'll give us wisdom if we ask for it, so ask for wisdom from God to show you what's causing you to put things off so much.

Then, set some rules and guidelines for yourself to help break that bad habit. Here are some quick cures for procrastination.

Suggested "Snooze Alarm" Gimmicks:
1. *Whatever you have to do today that you don't want to do, do it first*. I tell you, this works! I use it all the time. Often we procrastinate on the things we just don't like to do. But once we get those done, it frees up the rest of the day for us and increases our energy and motivation for other tasks.

As long as that unpleasant task hangs over our heads, we

mentally slow down because subconsciously we realize that the faster we work, the sooner we'll be forced to do the unpleasant job. Or we'll manufacture other busywork to avoid getting to that thing we don't want to do.

This one simple discipline could be life changing. I urge you to give it a try. Especially if you tend to be a habitual procrastinator, this will bring you great freedom and reduce your stress. Try it!

2. *Break your job up into small pieces.* I go into this in more detail in chapter seven, where we talk about staying on task. So I won't repeat those details here. But this is a major step forward in defeating the old monster, procrastination. I'm amazed at how many people have never learned this little trick, because it works so well. If you do one little piece today, and one tomorrow, and one the next day, before you know it, it's done.

As I write this, my house is for sale, and you know how it is when your home is on the market. You have to keep it picture perfect every day, because you never know when a realtor will show up with a prospective buyer. Well, my basement looked as if a tornado had struck. I had just kept piling things down there in storage, with no organization, and it looked terrible.

Until I put my home on the market, it didn't bother me. My philosophy is that what you can store in basements and shove in closets, out of sight, you don't have to worry about. Just keep the exterior looking good. (I hope that's not a comment on my character.) Now that people were going to be trudging through my basement, I knew I could no longer procrastinate.

So finally I set a schedule in my head that I would do one hour a night until it was done. Once I started, I finished in one night. It was not nearly as hard a job as I thought. Of course, I felt very good about myself once it was done.

When I think about the hours I sat on the sofa saying, "I've got to clean that basement soon," dreading it, imagining it to be much worse than it was, I realize again how procrastination robs you of time, energy and clear thinking. The longer you procrastinate, the worse the job seems.

If you will learn to break the job into small pieces, I promise it is a giant step forward in getting rid of this bad habit of putting things off.

3. *Start a job in the middle.* I think many of us procrastinate because we don't know how to start. I've learned that you don't have to start every job at the beginning and work to the end. Once you get started, it begins to happen. I think this is particularly helpful with mental jobs, like writing or planning or analyzing.

So often I start my writing project at some middle point. I have learned to simply get some words on the screen, and get them on fast. Don't wait for the brilliant first line or first paragraph. Just start it, anywhere, with any words, and it will start to happen. Often the first things I write are discarded, as the juices start to flow. But they get me started, and that is often the most difficult part.

Don't you find that once you start a job that seems so huge or so difficult, you discover it was not nearly as big or as difficult as you thought it would be? I believe this is almost always true.

> **Remember that your beginning doesn't have to be perfect.**

So remember that your beginning doesn't have to be perfect, nor do you have to approach a job from the top to the bottom. Use gimmicks like this simply to get you started. That's the hard part.

Thirty-Day Challenge

Once again, setting definite goals will help you implement these good work habits. Here's a suggested thirty-day plan.

Day 1: Determine which habits need to be improved:

☐ I need to work at being on time for every appointment and commitment.

☐ I need to return phone calls more promptly.

☐ I need to do a better job of keeping the commitments I make and becoming more dependable.

☐ I need to break the habit of procrastination.

If you have checked more than one, choose the one that is in greatest need of improvement and work on it for fifteen to thirty days, until you have it conquered. Then work on the others, one at a time.

If being on time is your problem, check the gimmicks suggested on pages 81–83 and put those in place right away. Practice them for at least thirty days.

If returning phone calls promptly is your challenge, decide right now that you will return all phone calls now pending, and you will heretofore return all phone calls within thirty minutes of receiving a message. Don't go easy on yourself. Make yourself do this for thirty days. You'll have a good new habit to replace the bad old one.

If you tend to overpromise or underdeliver, make a sign that says "Underpromise; overdeliver" and put it on your desk, computer, refrigerator or bulletin board. Write down every promise and commitment you make. Put them on your calendar. Check your calendar every day. In thirty days you can change your reputation from undependable to dependable with a little attention to this good work habit.

If you have a tendency to procrastinate, use the snooze alarm gimmicks outlined on pages 88–90, and force yourself to break this bad habit. After thirty days of avoiding this procrastination tendency, you are going to be so thrilled with the benefits that result, that you will be hooked! But remember, you have to hang in there for thirty days!

Other work habits are discussed in other chapters, like staying on task and being organized, because they are major areas of everyday discipline that need more elaboration. However, don't underestimate the power of these smaller work habits in your life. In fact, getting these in shape will go a long way toward imposing needed discipline in other major areas.

Six

When Your Desk Is a Disaster Zone!

THE DISCIPLINE OF BEING ORGANIZED

Suppose someone unknown by you was asked to describe you based on the condition of your office or work environment at this present moment. What would you look like? I certainly would not want that to happen to me. I'm afraid that unknown person would describe me as messy, unkempt, disorganized. As I write this chapter, we are two weeks from a major event in our ministry, and my desk and environs are in the "pile it up" stage.

For me this discipline is definitely seasonal—it comes and goes. At times I feel a burst of organizational drive, and it's amazing to see how much I can accomplish in short amounts of time. Just yesterday I went to Wal-Mart and bought several plastic storage boxes. I'm determined to get my closet looking as good as my sister-in-law's! Spring is not far away, so I must be entering the "spring" of my organizational season, and the

> Being organized is not perfectionism. It is not looking like a "neatnik."

"sap" for a neat, organized closet is beginning to drip.

At other times I have a "what does it matter?" attitude toward being organized. I try to convince myself that *looking* organized is not the same as *being* organized, so don't worry about the messy piles and stacks. You can't judge books by their covers, after all, and what matters is my productivity, so just keep working.

But the problem with that philosophy is that it gives me a license to be lazy about being organized, and being organized definitely does have something to do with my productivity. So we tackle—again—this discipline of imposing necessary organizational discipline on the daily routine.

What Organization Looks Like

Being organized is having enough order in your environment so that things can be easily located and maintained. It is being able to find what you need when you need it. It is the ability to walk through your home, office or workplace without tripping over "stuff." It's maintaining a mostly clutter-free environment.

Being organized is having a good sense of what you plan to do with your time each day. It means following some type of schedule and having a good sense of each day's priorities, deadlines, duties and commitments. It is the ability to avoid the "things falling through the cracks" syndrome.

> Organization also doesn't look the same on everyone!

Being organized is not perfectionism. It is not looking like a "neatnik." Nor is it the absence of all stacks or winning the prize for best housekeeper, cleanest desk or prettiest files.

Appearances are not the sole determining factor as to whether or not you are an organized person. Those of you who—like me—have an organized mind but an environment that appears disorganized breathe a sigh of relief, because it is possible to be organized and not look organized.

Organization also doesn't look the same on everyone! Some people need more structure and order than others. Some are more affected by the visual environment and its level of neatness than others. The litmus test is a matter of efficiency. Do you maximize your energy and efforts because you are organized, or are you wasting time, opportunities and resources because of some lack of basic daily organizational habits?

Do You Need to Be More Organized?

Here are some true-or-false questions that will help you determine whether this discipline is in good, fair or poor condition in your life.

TRUE FALSE

☐ ☐ I have a written agenda or "to do" list for each day.

☐ ☐ I have a filing or storage system that could be understood by others.

☐ ☐ If I were out of my office or workplace, an important document or other work effort could be found there by someone else without ripping the place apart.

☐ ☐ I spend less than ten minutes a day looking for something that I have misplaced.

☐ ☐ I have specific places for certain things, and I am careful to return things to their places.

☐ ☐ I can throw away things that are not necessary pretty easily; I'm not a "pack rat."

☐ ☐ I have a method of tracking the progress of any project in which I am involved. This includes deadlines, work efforts, progress reports or whatever is necessary to keep that project on target.

☐ ☐ My "stacks," if I have them, are organized; they are not just "piles." I know what is in a stack, and it is stacked where it is for a purpose.

☐ ☐ Rarely do important appointments or commitments or deadlines fall between the cracks with me.

☐ ☐ Most days I feel I have control of my schedule and begin with a clear idea of the priorities for that day.

SCORING:

9 or 10 True answers: You don't need to read this chapter.

5 to 8 True answers: Keep reading; you could use some help.

3 or 4 True answers: Read this chapter and find other reading material that goes into more detail on being organized.

1 or 2 True answers: Read on—and then go for help!

If your score indicates that you need to give this discipline some further thought, let's consider some key areas for discipline.

Organizing Your Daily Schedule

In Luke 14:28-30 Jesus took for granted that the man building a tower would have some method of organization; otherwise, the Master said, he'd look like a fool when his plans fell through. First the sensible builder would make sure he had enough money to complete the plan. No one with any wits would put in the foundation and *then* take a look at his finances.

It's the same with us. Charging into our tasks without knowing where we're going could be as futile as the efforts of a builder who just starts putting in a foundation without looking at his resources. We need to do some planning.

The time-management movement has spawned any number of daily planning systems that have been bought and used by millions. Obviously they have some value, and I am a proponent of some type of system that you use with consistency. It can be a simple daily list on a pad or calendar, which costs you practically nothing. If that is your preference, use the same pad, perhaps one with a different color from other pads, for your daily to-do lists.

If you choose to purchase one of the many planning systems, remember that it only works if you use it. Just buying it does not magically make you organized! Some people feel that by making a significant investment in such a system, they are more motivated to use it. If so, fine. The point is, develop a system for writing down each day's duties, responsibilities, appointments, deadlines, etc., and use it every day.

I would not recommend self-stick notes for this purpose. One person who worked for me used this method to keep track of her "to do" items. She stuck them all around her desk, but I noticed that she often failed to meet her deadlines because she had failed to notice the note! Those little pieces of paper can easily be lost. It is best to list your "to dos" all together on one piece of paper that is recognizable and easy to find.

That also allows you to prioritize your activities much better. One familiar method is the ABC priority system, where you categorize your "to do" items by letter:

A = the most important things, must be done today.

B = things that must be done this week.

C = anything with a deadline later than this week or an optional item.

Here are some other helpful hints for to-do lists:

- *Establish a daily time for writing this list.* Some people like to write down tomorrow's "to dos" at the end of today. I find that helpful because then I have a clear view of what tomorrow holds for me. Others prefer writing it down first thing in the morning. The important thing is to develop a habit of doing it consistently at a certain time each day.
- *As you write your daily list, group similar tasks as much as possible to avoid as much set up time as you can.* For example, group all those phone calls you need to make and try to do them all at one time.
- *Whenever you make a commitment for a future date, put that commitment on your calendar at once.*
- *Include long-term goals and activities as well as short-term ones.* Remember, long-term goals have to become a part of a daily plan, or they'll always be long-term and never accomplished. So plan to do at least a small part of your long-term goals each day or week, and you'll eventually get there.
- *Be flexible.* Often our days don't go as we hoped or planned, and we have to be prepared for rescheduling, redefining or removing something from our list.

One last thought about these daily planning lists. Don't become paranoid about doing everything on your list. That list is something of a "wish list"; it represents what you would like to accomplish on a given day, if all goes well and Murphy doesn't

> I was prone to overestimate what I could do in one day. So I heaped unnecessary stress on myself by my obsession with marking everything off of my list.

kick in. But most days are not that controllable, and there are interruptions, divine appointments, unplanned meetings and all kinds of things that interfere with our routine.

I used to feel like a failure when I didn't accomplish everything on my list. And I was prone to overestimate what I could do in one day. So I heaped unnecessary stress on myself by my obsession with marking everything off of my list. It was almost like a contest with me, and I felt the need to "win" every day by proving that I could do it all. Well, a few years and a little maturity have helped me have a more realistic view of my schedule and my time.

As a believer in Jesus Christ, it is also important for me to remember that he is ultimately in control. Sure, he expects me to be a good steward of my time, and being organized is therefore important. The Bible says that "everything should be done in a fitting and orderly way" (1 Cor 14:40). But he has a right to change my schedule, to alter my plans, to divert my attention.

This has been and continues to be a lesson for me to learn. Being a controlling person, I don't like those "divine appointments" that take me off course. Yet many times I've had the most wonderful experiences when someone or something interrupted my day. God had his own list for me, and he replaced mine with something better.

Organizing Your "Stuff"

First let's define the difference between stacks and piles:

- *Stacks* are accumulations of related information in one specific place.
- *Piles* are dumping grounds for unrelated items because we don't know where else to put them.

This is where the neatnik or perfectionist will have some difficulty, but the truth is, you can have a disorganized look without being disorganized. Or to put it more positively, you can be organized without looking organized.

Some years ago a wonderful young woman worked for me who operated from stacks. Her system was to keep every current project out and in view until that project was completed. She would often have stacks all over her office, but she knew exactly what was in each stack; it was there for a purpose; and in her mind it was not at all confusing. Once that project was completed, the stack then was placed in appropriate files with clearly marked labels in a very organized manner.

If the appearance of her office had been important, I might have encouraged her to redesign her system, because at times it didn't look very neat. But there was not an image issue in our small office, since we don't have very much outside traffic coming in, so I felt there was no need to disturb her highly efficient system. It worked beautifully for her.

> If your work environment is cluttered with piles, it saps a great deal of your energy and mental capacity because of the confusion it causes.

Another staff member operates just the opposite. Nothing is out on her desk except what she is working on at the moment. She has a good filing system and can't stand to see things stacked around her. For her, that is confusing, so she puts things away regularly and brings them out only when needed. Her system takes more get-out and put-away time, but it keeps her mind from being cluttered.

I find I have a certain tolerance level for clutter or stacks, and then I go into action. At a particular point when I reach that "high water" mark, my mind starts spinning from the clutter, and I recognize that the stacks have become piles and something has to be done now!

You see, if your work environment is cluttered with piles, it saps a great deal of your energy and mental capacity because of the confusion it causes. It's like letting your computer memory become so cluttered with all kinds of stuff that you can't store anything else until you clean it out.

Stacks become piles when you're afraid to look through that pile because you're not sure what is there, and it may be something very important that you've forgotten!

How many clothes are hanging in your closet that you have not worn in a year? If there are more than one or two items, you need to clean out that closet. I keep hanging on to clothes, convincing myself I'll lose weight and get back into it again someday, or maybe next week I'll want to wear it. Then, years pass and I realize I haven't touched that garment.

There are so many needy people who could wear our good clothes that are just cluttering up our closets. Most of us have far too many clothes, and it would be a wonderful thing to share from our abundance with those who are truly needy. If we give away everything that we haven't worn in one year, that will probably empty our closets by 25 percent. Then, using those purchased bins, stack things in a more orderly way and keep like objects together. (The "spring cleaning" bug has bit me, even though it is snowing outside as I write!)

Often I find that I forget I have some piece of clothing because it gets squeezed between other garments, and I can't see it is there, so it just hangs for weeks or months, unused. Recently I discovered a brand new pair of shoes that I bought on sale out of season and put in the back of my closet, only to forget them entirely. They had been there for a couple of years, waiting to be worn!

Start Small

I keep saying this about every discipline, but this is a key to your success in implementing any new one, and that is, start small. If you need to be more organized about your time and work effort, don't overwhelm yourself with fancy systems right off the bat. Start with a simple list, prioritize it and set a thirty-day trial period.

Thirty-Day Challenge

Day 1:
Decide what you need to do to become more organized:

_____ I need to begin using a daily planning system.

_____ I need to go through all the "piles" on my desk and in my home, throwing away what is no longer useful and organizing what I want to keep.

Follow the plan that will help you accomplish your goal.

Day 2 (daily planning): Choose the planning system that will work best for you. Keep it simple and inexpensive if you are first starting to use a planning system. A simple week-at-a-glance calendar may be adequate. Then set a time of day to add to and update your planning system each day, and develop the good habit of referring to this system regularly throughout your day.

Day 2 (organizing): Set up a schedule for getting through your "piles" and organizing them. It would be a good idea to put this plan in writing—a part of your new planning system perhaps! (You can do this in conjunction with implementing a new daily planning system, if indeed you need to work on both areas of organization.)

Days 3–30 (daily planning): It's very important that you stick with this new planning system for at least thirty days, because the first few days will be annoying. At first it seems to take more time because it's a new habit and you have to think about it. But impose that discipline for thirty days, and by then you'll be able to assess its value to you. If you give up quickly, you'll never know the benefits from having a daily planning system.

Days 3–30 (organizing): Organize one stack, one closet, one room per day or week until you've gotten through all your "piles." Buy whatever containers you need to be able to organize what you intend to keep.

If, after thirty days, it hasn't improved your ability to organize your day, evaluate if it was your fault or the system just wasn't the right one. No system will work if you don't stick with it. But I firmly believe that different people need different systems. It's not one size fits all. So keep tweaking it until you come up with the right method for you that truly helps you organize and prioritize your time and duties.

You'll know it's right when you are less stressful; when you don't lie awake at night wondering what you forgot; when you don't wake up in the middle of the night in a cold sweat because you remember what you forgot; when you realize that being "in control" brings a great deal of satisfaction and enjoyment that you had been missing before.

Tackle one clutter at a time. Take a room a week in your home, or a closet a week, or even a drawer a week until you get it organized. It may take a long time if things are really in bad shape, but you'll be encouraged when you see some progress, and that will help you to keep on keepin' on.

Take on one pile at a time. It could be the piles on your desk or in your closets, or the piles in your basement or garage. But if you will think of it as a pile at a time, that's a lot more manageable than the whole thing.

I'm convinced that once you begin to implement some discipline in this area of being more organized, the benefits are going to be so obvious and so delightful, that you'll be highly motivated to finish the job. Discipline begets discipline, and success feeds on success. So, start small, and expect a miracle!

Seven

When You Get Bored Easily!

THE DISCIPLINE OF STAYING ON TASK

I've decided to write this chapter out of sequence because I'm once again having trouble staying on task. So I need to read what I'm going to write about this. Maybe it will help me stay on task and finish this book.

Do you have trouble with this one? This is a daily discipline that drives me up the wall. "I have a short attention span" is one way to put it. Another way is "I get restless very easily." Besides, any one task gets boring after a while; I'm looking for something more invigorating to hold my attention.

When I think about it, I'm amazed that I've written any books or managed to complete any task, because I really hate to stay on task. It gets harder as I get older. So if you struggle with this discipline, believe me, you have my sympathy and my empathy, and you can be sure I'm not going to lay any guilt trips on you in this chapter.

> Staying with a job until it is completed is one of the best time-management techniques anyone has come up with.

I said that eating right was one of my two toughest disciplines, and this is the second one!

What makes it so difficult to stay on task? For me, it is truly a restless personality and a big lazy streak. I like activity, but I don't like the same activity for long periods of time. Staying on task, sticking with the stuff until the job gets done, takes discipline.

The Importance of Staying on Task

Staying with a job until it is completed is one of the best time-management techniques anyone has come up with. Jumping from one thing to another, leaving work half done, procrastinating about the finishing touches, keeping too many balls in the air—all of these are ready-made disasters for productivity and effectiveness.

A person who develops the ability to stay on task and move a job as far as possible before going on to something else rises to the top in any organization. The on-task person has less stress than the rest of us, sleeps better at night, is less frazzled and hassled and is far more focused and composed.

I believe this is a discipline that has been largely overlooked by many people. You see, we can fool ourselves so easily into thinking we're productive and effective by simply being busy. So if I flit from one project to another unnecessarily, jumping around to avoid boredom or whatever, I may put on a good appearance, but I'm really wasting time.

> We can fool ourselves so easily into thinking we're productive and effective by simply being busy.

In fact, let's face it—many of us flit around like butterflies in order to give the appearance of being very important and very busy. In our culture, busyness equals status and respect. So the busier we appear to be, the more valuable and important we seem. Flitting butterflies can fool others as well as themselves into thinking they are the busiest creatures on earth!

Much of our productivity is consumed with starting up and shutting down. As I flit from one project to another, I have to readjust my working situation, get out new equipment, files, research, and then I have to switch mentally from one thing to another. All that switching tends to waste both time and creativity.

In any factory environment, one of the highest goals for productivity that will improve the bottom line is to run the machinery without interruption as long as possible. For example, a printer who wants to maximize profit will seek the kind of work that fits his equipment best, and then he'll try to line up his work in such a way that he minimizes the down time of the printing presses.

Southwest Airlines has built a lot of its success on minimiz-

> ## By staying on task, we minimize our down time and our set-up time.

ing the downtime of their airplanes. They turn their planes around faster than anyone else, and that means those expensive planes are spending less time on the ground, where they're bringing in no revenue, and more time in the air, where they are generating revenue. Pretty smart business strategy.

By staying on task, we minimize our down time and our set-up time. It really makes a difference in performance when we start to really focus on staying on task.

Common "Flitting" Excuses

I have developed some incredibly good excuses for ignoring this needed discipline of staying on task. I probably have better excuses than anyone I know. Here are some:

"I just don't have the creative juices flowing today, so it's really a waste of time to continue to do this until that magical state of creativity again descends upon me." This is my favorite excuse, and I use it frequently. But you know, it's just self-deception. I know that those of you who are required to do creative things can relate to this. There certainly are days when the writing comes easier than others, but those good days are few and far between. I'd never meet my deadlines if I only wrote when I felt "creative," whatever that is.

I remember asking Babbie Mason, the wonderful singer and songwriter, how she came up with new ideas for her songs. I said, "Do you just have

Inspiration is mostly perspiration.

moments of great inspiration when you sit at the piano and the whole song just pours out of you as fast as you can write it down?" She laughed and said she wished it were that way. But song writing, she said, was just plain hard work. It is sitting at the piano for hours, sometimes, trying to get one line right.

I'm convinced that few of us are creative in bursts of inspiration. But rather inspiration comes as we begin the job and stick with it until it is finished. Sometimes I'll get an emotional surge of inspiration about a message, and at that moment I think it's the best idea I've ever had. I can't wait to get to my computer and flesh it out. But more often than not, those "flashes" peter out quickly. They rarely end up being the marvelous, inspired messages I thought they would be.

Inspiration is mostly perspiration. You've probably heard that before, but I want to reinforce it. It is my guess that many of you reading this book have the capability of being far more "creative" than you've ever imagined, but you keep thinking that you need some special gene or gift or personality. Believe me, the creativity comes as you begin to do it.

Jesus taught us that when we use what we have, he gives us more to use. The parable of the talents, as found in Matthew 25:14-30, is very clear on this. As the two profitable servants used the resources they had, the master gave them more to use.

> We can be masterful at self-deception when it comes to avoiding doing what we should do but we don't want to do.

If you want to be more creative than you are, then start using the gifts you have now, and ask God to multiply your gifts.

Waiting for bursts of creativity is a guaranteed path to lack of productivity. It takes discipline to stick with a task until you've reached your goal, and I promise you, that is more important than "inspiration."

"I need to get all these other little things cleared up before I can finish this task." When I reach my boredom point in any job, I'm looking for excuses to quit. Often I will notice some other project or jobs that are on my desk and convince myself that I must stop now and do something else. This is my "higher priority" excuse, and it really seems legitimate at the time.

Let's face it: We can be masterful at self-deception when it comes to avoiding doing what we should do but we don't want to do. After all, that's what discipline is all about and why it is no fun. But it's at those moments we have to remind ourselves that the fruits of discipline are worth the pain.

"I was so good yesterday that I deserve a break today." I'm big on rewards to keep me motivated. But sometimes I'm *too* big on them. Yes, it's good to give yourself a break for good behavior, but let's not go overboard! It takes very little in the way of staying on task for me to decide that I'm eligible for a big reward.

Let go of the reins of control and allow people to do their jobs on their own.

"I'll put in extra time on this tomorrow [or next week or next month], so I can stop now." I use this one far too often. When I want to quit what I'm now doing before reaching my predetermined goals, I just tell myself that I'll make up for it tomorrow—or whenever. And I fully intend to do that. But tomorrow I discover I have the same problem with staying on task, and now I need to stay on task even longer, which is even more difficult.

"If I don't stop and do this other task, something will go wrong. My staff [or coworker or family or friend] needs my attention and help right now!" This falls into the "the world will stop revolving without me" category. I'm learning how to let go of the reins of control and allow people to do their jobs on their own. Being a "control freak" has created some difficulties for me. Often this control tendency will pop into my mind as I'm intent on completing a job and cause me to think that I must stop now and interact with others so they will do their jobs correctly.

Now, it's true that as a manager of people, I need to be accessible and available. But I also need to let those people do their jobs without me looking over their shoulders too often. It is humbling to recognize that people can keep going even when I'm not there to direct, but that's the truth. I'm not nearly as

> Setting up small but frequent rewards is very important for those of us who are attention-span challenged.

indispensable as I think I am!

You don't have to work in a managerial position to learn that truth. Land in the hospital, and you'll see that your family can make do without you. Have a day when you can't help out your best friend, and she may do just fine on her own. God hasn't made you the only capable person in the world!

Well, these are some of my favorite excuses for deceiving myself and allowing myself to get off-task and go back to "flitting." But I want to tell you that I'm better than I used to be. That's not saying much, I know, but it is encouraging to see that I can improve in this discipline, because if I can, anyone can.

Suggested "Snooze Alarm" Gimmicks

For those who find it a challenge, here are some gimmicks that I use just about every day of my life to keep me on task. For the most part, when I implement them, they work:

1. *Divide your job into reasonable sections and set goals for each section.* We're back to that baby-step approach, and this is a big help for those of us who are mentally challenged by staying on

task. If a job looks too big to me, if I can't see light at the end of the tunnel, then I'm likely to quit where I am.

I've never written a book, but I have written chapters. To think of writing a book overwhelms me. So I always think of the chapter that I need to write. Of course, I'm smart enough to know that chapters make books, but this mental gymnastic is an absolute essential for me. I would never get started if I thought I had to write a book, but somehow I figure all I have to write is a chapter today, and that seems possible.

Another way to do this would be to allocate a certain amount of time to the task. For example, spend all morning on a job and then move on to something else. I use that occasionally, too, but frankly I've found myself frittering away the hours, then when noon comes, I say, well I reached that goal, I can quit, when in reality I didn't use that time so well and could have done more. I became a clock-watcher, rather than a job doer. So, generally it works better for me to set a work-progress goal and stick with it until I get there.

2. *Set up small benchmarks for small rewards.* Setting up small but frequent rewards is very important for those of us who are attention-span challenged. For example, I say to myself, "OK, you've got to write this chapter today, but if you will stay on task for the next two hours without stopping, then you can take a break, get something to drink, make a phone call and have a ten-minute sabbatical."

As I write this down on paper for all to read, I'm beginning to realize how stupid it may sound to some. How could a fairly intelligent woman live her life in what may seem like self-deception? Why can't I be mature enough or professional enough to just set the task out before me and do it, without these mental gyrations? How could a thinking woman continue to fool herself in the same ways day after day?

I don't know, folks. All I know is, I have found some things that work for me, and I'm not going to delve a lot deeper into the psychology of it all. I want to reach my goals. I have lots to accomplish. I really want to do many things. I'll never succeed unless I make myself stay on task and get the job done. So whatever it takes, as long as it's not immoral or illegal, I'm willing to do it, no matter how stupid I may look.

Maybe that's a secret of becoming a more disciplined person, when it doesn't come easily. Maybe you have to be willing to make a fool out of yourself if necessary. No, I think I'll say *when* necessary, because it seems to me that, except for those naturally disciplined people who really don't have to give it much thought, the rest of us in varying degrees have to learn how to fool ourselves into doing what we know we have to do to be successful.

3. *Try to get rid of distractions.* Telephones, conversations, sunlight pouring in the window and luring you outside, and stacks of other projects all around you, reminding you of other things that need to be done—all of these are trying to keep you from staying on task. You need to eliminate as many as possible.

One way to control the telephone is to set a time period—say, one hour—that you will not take or make calls, and let the voice mail do that work for you. Telephones are probably our most common interruption, and while we cannot ignore them or control them completely, we can use some of our modern technology to group those calls as much as possible. (Be careful not to abuse those voice mail and answering machine capabilities, however. It can become a very annoying habit to those who need to reach you, and it can make their jobs more difficult.)

On the job, shutting your office door, if you have one, turning your desk away from the traffic flow, putting up a "Do not disturb" sign, avoiding eye contact as people walk by—all of these can help to minimize those costly interruptions when you are trying to stay on task. Advise your boss that you intend to get a certain work effort done by a certain time, so that perhaps he or she will be cooperative in giving you that uninterrupted time.

At home, turn off the television. Some of us—and I put myself in that category—just keep that box blasting out too much. We singles tend to turn it on for company, to hear another voice in the house. I find I can become distracted at something on the tube and waste a half hour before I know it.

Think about the unnecessary interruptions in your day. What causes them? A candy dish on your desk will bring people to you in droves. You might want to move it while you're trying to stay on task. Being located too near certain things—like copiers and faxes—can cause you to become the resident supply room for whatever is needed by whoever is using the equipment. Keeping those areas well stocked may help eliminate some of those unnecessary interruptions.

But mostly watch out for your self-interruptions. If you think of something you need to do, make a note of it instead of stopping to do it right that minute. Group your phone calls and try to do them all at one time as much as possible, instead of making several calls as they come to mind. And use your frequent reward stops as your breaks for food and drink.

Please let me know if you have some great ideas for staying on task, because I'm always looking for more help in this area. But I can assure you that I am much better at it than I used to be. The benefits of imposing this discipline have become so apparent to me that I'm hooked. I am convinced of its importance, and that is a great motivation. So, please impose these "snooze alarm" gimmicks long enough to see what they will do for you. Once you see the results, it makes it easier to stay on task!

Thirty-Day Challenge

Day 1: Analyze your "to-do list" for the day or week. Use the planning techniques that were discussed in the last chapter to prioritize your work or duties, and determine how much time you will need for each task. Assign hours of the day and days of the week for each needed task.

Day 2: Look at your assignments for the day. Set work-progress goals for each thing that you need to do. Determine in advance what progress you need to make before you stop. Set up some rewards for yourself upon reaching your predetermined goals.

Examples:
As soon as I complete this task, I will take a snack break.

   When I have made this much progress (be very specific), I can do ____ (something you really want to do).

Days 3–30: Continue each day with goal-setting and rewards for staying with the job until you've reached your goals. Don't be discouraged with failure. Start over the next day. Of course, each day that you fail to reach your performance goals makes the next day more difficult. So, really push yourself to stay on task each day. But think of it as a day at a time.

Remind yourself of the gimmicks we covered to help you avoid interruptions. Take control of those interruptions in your work effort as much as you possibly can. Be proactive rather than reactive.

After thirty days of practicing this discipline, you are going to be enjoying great freedom and a wonderful sense of accomplishment—freedom from the guilt and worry and stress that comes when we leave jobs unfinished. And a good feeling about yourself because you stuck to your plan and made it happen. That will motivate you to continue this good habit of staying on task.

Others will begin to notice the difference in your productivity and accomplishments and the difference in your attitude. The side benefits of staying on task and completing your jobs in a timely manner will astonish you. Be prepared for some wonderful surprises that come your way when you conquer this discipline.

Eight

When You're Too Busy to Get to Know God!

THE DISCIPLINE OF DAILY DEVOTIONS

Does this sound familiar?

You set your clock at night with very good intentions to spend some time with the Lord before hurrying off to your busy day. You want to be a victorious Christian, and you know that a consistent time of daily devotions is essential. It seems to be a difficult habit for you to establish, but you're going to try again.

Somehow that alarm goes off much earlier than you expected, and after delaying the inevitable for ten minutes, you crawl out of bed and start the day. In a few moments you find your Bible and sit down to have your devotions.

Now, where will you begin? Guess you could start to read the Bible through, but those Old Testament books get pretty difficult. Or you could use the "open Bible" method; you know, open the Bible and read whatever you find. Well, your

> When we spend daily time getting to know God, pouring out our hearts to him in prayer, it transforms us into the likeness of Jesus Christ.

time is running short, so you decide to read a psalm. Now, a quick prayer before you finish.

"Dear Lord," you begin, "thanks for this day and all your blessings. Please bless me today and my family...," and you try to pray. It seems you can't get too far without your thoughts wandering. You think of what you've got to do that day, you feel yourself getting sleepy and you struggle to get through your prayer. After a few moments of "blessing" everyone who comes to your mind, you look at the clock and realize you'd better get moving or you're going to be late.

Daily devotions—wow, they just don't seem to work for you. You know you should, you try, but consistency just never materializes. It seems like such a drudgery, and you end up feeling guilty.

If that rings a bell with you, let me assure you that I don't know of any Christian who hasn't struggled with establishing a meaningful, consistent devotional life. You're not alone! For many Christians—perhaps most—it seems like a heavy duty instead of a great privilege.

This discipline gives us difficulty because it is the most powerful discipline we can ever impose in our lives. When we spend daily time getting to know God, hearing his voice, pouring out our hearts to him in prayer, and realigning our thinking with

the Word of God regularly, it trans-
forms us into the likeness of Jesus
Christ with ever-increasing glory, to
quote the words from 2 Corinthians
3:18, and we become more and more

> **When I neglect a daily time with God, the other daily disciplines of my life suffer.**

powerful in the kingdom. Therefore, the enemy of our souls
fights us on this discipline more than any other.

For me, all the other disciplines in this book begin here.
When I neglect a daily time with God, the other daily disciplines of my life suffer. In this quiet time alone with Almighty
God, I find the motivation and power to do what I know I
should do. Without the inner strength that is imparted to me
in this time with God, I'm back to my old lazy, self-seeking,
undisciplined me quicker than you can believe!

What Does It Mean to Know God?

It might be helpful to refer to this daily time as a time to get to
know God. It should certainly be a devotional time and a quiet
time, but the purpose is to get to know God better. The
psalmist said, "Be still, and know that I am God" (Ps 46:10).

Getting to know God is nothing mysterious. It is the same
as getting to know anyone better. The better you know someone, the better you know:

> To know God means that we become increasingly aware
> of who he is, how he thinks,
> what he would tell us to do in any situation.

- what that individual thinks about different subjects.
- how he or she reacts to different situations.
- what that person likes—his or her personality and character.
- his or her past, history and background.

You've heard couples who have been married for many years say that they know what their partners are thinking without asking. If you have children, you probably know just how they're going to react in a situation before it ever happens! Why? Because you've spent so much time with those people, gone through so many experiences together, observed them so often, that you know them inside out.

Well, God in his great mercy has made it possible for us to know him. Because of Jesus, we can know his viewpoint on any subject. We can know what he's done in the past, and that tells us how he will be in the future. We can intimately know his nature, what he's like. To know God means that we become increasingly aware of who he is, how he thinks, what he would tell us to do in any situation. To know God means to see the world through his eyes, to have his perspective on what's happening.

My friend, if you will just think about that for a few

moments, your mind will probably blow a few fuses, because it's almost more than we can comprehend. To think that the God of all the universe will allow us to know him!

> God has promised that we will find him when we seek him with our whole hearts.

I remind you that any person who sets out to know God will never be disappointed, because God has promised that we *will* find him when we seek him with our whole hearts (see Jer 29:13).

Jesus said, "Now this is eternal life: that they may know you, the only true God, and Jesus Christ, whom you have sent" (Jn 17:3). The apostle Paul wrote "I want to know Christ and the power of his resurrection and the fellowship of sharing in his sufferings, becoming like him in his death" (Phil 3:10).

Knowing God is the most important pursuit of any person's life, and it is a pursuit that requires discipline. No, it's not a duty, it's a privilege, but like many privileges, it requires our co-operation and commitment.

What Does It Take to Build a Relationship?

If you want to know someone better, you have to really want to. Then you have to put feet to your desires and become very intentional about building that relationship. It will require a high level of commitment on your part. That means it will take up a good bit of your time. The more you want to know some-

> Our knowledge of God will depend on how much we are willing to do the things required to build the relationship.

one, the more time it will take. That, in turn, may have some effect on your schedule and cause you to make some decisions about what you will exclude from your schedule in order to make time to build this relationship. But if you really want to know that person, you will be willing to make those changes.

Think of a time when you were "in love." Was it hard to find hours in your schedule for that loved one? Didn't you gladly make all kinds of changes to your schedule in order to be with that person? You see, when we really want to get to know someone, making time for it is no chore; it is a joy.

Our knowledge of God will depend on how much we are willing to do the things required to build the relationship. That willingness indicates how much we really want to know God.

Psalm 42:1-2 describes the heart of a person who truly wants to know God: "As the deer pants for streams of water, so my soul pants for you, O God. My soul thirsts for God, for the living God."

Most of us are probably not too familiar with deer, but if you've ever had dogs, you know how they pant for water, especially on a hot day. Their tongues hang out and their mouths gape open, waiting to get to the water dish. You can imagine that the deer in the mountains don't stray too far from their water source, for they pant for that water. The psalmist uses this illustration from nature to describe how he desires to know God.

Now, if you can honestly say that you truly want to get to know God,

Choose a time of day that will work best for you.

that your soul pants for God, then the next thing is to find a method and structure that will help you. If you're willing to make the time commitment and impose the necessary discipline, then the only thing lacking is finding a way to do it.

When Is the Best Time to Get to Know God?

One practical question that arises when we start considering a daily time with God is when will we do it. It will be necessary to impose a schedule for this, to set aside a certain time of day that will be best for you. If you leave that too flexible, you'll find that most days will go by without your quiet time with God, because all kinds of other things will crowd into your day. After all, you have an enemy of your soul who will go into high gear when he realizes you're serious about getting to know God, and filling up your time is one of his best tricks. Therefore, it is good to choose a time of day that will work best for you.

Consider these passages:

- "Satisfy us in the morning with your unfailing love, that we may sing for joy and be glad all our days" (Ps 90:14).

> ## Spending time with God before the day begins
> ## makes us much better prepared for the day ahead.

- "In the morning, O Lord, you hear my voice; in the morning I lay my requests before you and wait in expectation" (Ps 5:3).
- "Let the morning bring me word of your unfailing love, for I have put my trust in you. Show me the way I should go, for to you I lift up my soul" (Ps 143:8).

Other passages also indicate that morning is a good time to spend with God. I think for most of us it is the best choice because we have more control over those morning hours (if we get up early enough). And spending time with God before the day begins makes us much better prepared for the day ahead. Also, there is a biblical principle of giving God the firstfruits of our lives—the best part, not leftovers. Most of us are more alert, less distracted and more focused in the morning than later in the day, when our brains are somewhat fried!

For these reasons, I suggest you find a morning time with God if at all possible. But if you honestly can make it work better in the evenings, of course that's fine. Choose what works best for you, but by all means, choose a time. You'll never have a consistent devotional life until you have a specific time designated for it.

You may be wondering how much time you need to set

aside. Well, I can't answer that question for anyone except myself, so you also will have to answer for yourself. Nor do I believe that what I do is necessarily what everyone should do. I have more control over my time than a great many of you do. Because I'm single with no small children, I can get up when I please, and I don't have

> It will be difficult to have any meaningful communication with God if you only give him a five- or ten-minute daily time slot!

to worry about other family members. With that luxury and freedom, I feel I am more responsible for a significant time commitment than, say, a working mom who rarely has a moment to herself.

The guiding principle is that to whom much is given, much is required. We all have the same number of hours in a day, but for some of us there are more discretionary hours than for others. However, it will be difficult to have any meaningful communication with God if you only give him a five- or ten-minute daily time slot! Your time commitment needs to be as significant as you can possibly make it.

Perhaps you'll need to get creative about finding that time. Moms can do it while babies sleep or while they are washing dishes or doing laundry or driving to the soccer game. There is much time in our day that is mentally wasted, where we could train ourselves to use that time for prayer and meditation, listening to recorded Scripture, etc.

Be warned of this: Many things will start to happen to try to destroy or interrupt this time you've set aside. Maybe you've decided to get up early before other family members rise. Don't be surprised if someone else in the family gets up at the same time, though he or she has never done it before! Some of you will have sudden job pressures and workloads that demand extra time, and you'll be tempted to forgo the time with God. You may discover that it's so much harder to wake up each morning than it used to be. Sleep may overtake you more easily than before.

You can count on some obstacles being thrown in your path now that you've made a commitment. I've never seen it fail. Just remember, that's the enemy of your soul trying to discourage you and keep you from establishing this wonderful new habit. He knows if you get serious about getting to know God, he's in trouble, and he doesn't give up without a fight. Just be prepared, and be resolute in your commitment, regardless of his tactics.

What Is the Best Method to Use in Getting to Know God?

There are two parts to getting to know God:

1. Listening to what he has to say to you.
2. Talking to him.

These are done, for the most part, through Bible reading, study, meditation and prayer. If you have not already "fallen in love" with the Word of God, that will undoubtedly be one of the results of your quest to know God. Job said, "I have treasured the words of his mouth more than my daily bread" (Jb 23:12). That will happen to you, too, the more you get into this incredible Book. It will be more important to you than food. You won't be able to imagine a day without it. Your Bible will be marked and frayed at the edges, but you'll hang on to it long after you should have bought a new one because it has become so familiar and dear.

For reading and meditating on God's Word, I would not recommend the "open Bible" method—just opening the Bible and reading whatever appears before your eyes! That's like going to the kitchen cupboard, closing your eyes and grabbing something to eat. While it may be better than nothing at all, your diet will not be very well-balanced and probably not that tasty! You'll also end up eating inappropriate foods for the time of day—like navy beans for breakfast!

There are many good ways to systematically read the Word of God. I'm going to give you three suggestions and indicate the method I use and why. But the important thing is that you find a method that suits you, that it be planned and that you stick to it.

Method #1

Choose one book (or portion of a larger book) and read that entire book every day for one month. For instance, the book of Ephesians has six chapters and could easily be read in one sitting. If you read Ephesians every day for one month, you'd really become familiar with the truth in that book. It would be indelibly entered into your mental computer.

I think this is an excellent thing to do, but I would also combine it with other readings in the Bible to have a balanced diet. For instance, read the book of Ephesians every day along with a chapter in one of the Gospels and a chapter or two from the Old Testament.

Method #2

Read the Bible through from beginning to end in one year. Many people do this, and it's certainly a good idea. You can get published guides as to how much to read each day in order to cover it in one year. They are available in any Christian bookstore. In fact, there is a Bible that is designed to help you read it through in one year, divided into suggested readings for each day. These guides give you a balanced diet of Old and New Testament each day, and I think that has some merit.

Method #3

On a daily basis:

- *Read one chapter from a Gospel.* Start in Matthew, go through John, and start again in Matthew.
- *Read one chapter from the remainder of the New Testament.* Start in Acts, go through Revelation, then start again in Acts.

- *Read one Psalm.* Start at Psalm 1, go through Psalm 150, and start over again.
- *Read one chapter from Proverbs.* There are thirty-one chapters, so it's easy to match the chapter with the day of the month.
- *Read two other Old Testament chapters.* Start at Genesis and go through Job, then start again in Genesis. Start in Ecclesiastes and go through Malachi, then start again in Ecclesiastes.

This is the method I have devised for myself. I like it because it keeps me going through the entire Bible, but it also keeps me focused on the words and life of Jesus at all times, as well as the praise nature of the Psalms and the practical, everyday guidelines I gain from Proverbs. I keep a card in my Bible that lists the last chapters read, so I'll know where to start each day.

Choose from these, combine them into one of your own, or come up with your own unique plan. The important thing is to read a good portion every day, to make sure it is a balanced diet from all parts of the Scripture, to keep track and be consistent. *But most of all, read it!*

Meditating on the Word of God

Meditation is in ill-repute in some Christian circles these days, with all the Eastern religions focusing on it as though through

> We need to learn the art of meditating on the Word of God.

sheer meditation one can find life's answers. While we certainly do not ascribe to that philosophy of meditation, we need to learn the art of meditating on the Word of God. We live in a society where quiet thinking is often considered a waste of time. For me, it is a continual retraining of my mind to learn that time spent in quiet thoughts about God's Word is profitable time.

Here are some ideas to help you develop the art of meditating on the Word of God.

- As you read, if you're like most of us, there will be times when your concentration factor will be zero! When I catch myself reading but not knowing what I've read, I make myself go back and reread that portion. Then I say to myself, "What did you read? What does it mean? What does it say to you?" This facilitates the meditation process—causes me to rethink and reconsider what I've just read.

- Another good method to help develop a meditative reading style is to focus on your state of mind before you begin to read. One thing that works well for me is to tell myself to read today as though I've never heard or read this before in my whole life, it's all new to me, and I'm reading it for the first time. We often need clearer eyesight as we read God's Word to keep from reading things into it that are not there or missing things that are there. This helps me very much to read the Scripture in a meditative state of mind.

Time spent in quiet thoughts about God's Word is profitable time.

- When I'm reading the Gospels, I try to put myself in the shoes of the people in the story. I often think, "How would I have reacted if I'd been there when Jesus did that or said that?" As you start to read your chapter in the Gospels, say to yourself, "Put yourself in their place. You are one of the crowd [or one of the disciples, or the blind man or one of the Pharisees], and this Jesus has just burst on your world. If you heard these words for the first time right from the man himself, what would you think, what would you do?"

So much of what Jesus did and said is absolutely phenomenal, and we need to capture and keep that wonder and awe at his power and his words. Again, this works really well for me. I always look forward to the Gospels, because Jesus is so exciting and revolutionary. And I never read without seeing something I've never seen before.

- Another good idea is to stop in the middle of a passage and pray about it as it speaks to your heart. Ask yourself, "Do you really believe this is the truth? If you do, how does it affect you?"

- One key element to help in meditation and focus is the location you choose for this quiet time. For me, I have a spot in my house that has become my "quiet time" spot. All my

> ## This is our daily feeding time,
> ## when we gain nourishment to get us through the day.

devotional-type books are there, and it represents meditation to me. In fact, I rarely sit on that chair in that room at any other time. I thought I was a little crazy until I read that Charles Haddon Spurgeon, the great English preacher, did the same thing! I have also used airplanes, hotel lobbies and other unlikely spots as the occasion demanded!

Occasionally some passage speaks to me so powerfully that I read no further for the day. Rather, I sit and think and write and consider what impact this message is to have on my life.

Recently as I was reading I became overwhelmed with the thought that God loves me. Now, I've known that from my earliest years, but in a new way, which is really beyond my ability to describe, the truth that the God of all the universe loves me took hold of my heart and mind with such power that I could not move for a long time. I sat and meditated on those three words, and my heart was refreshed and encouraged and blessed beyond belief. Even now as I write of it, the emotions come flooding back, and I am again overwhelmed with the fact that God loves me. Had I not spent that quiet time getting to know God that day, meditating on his Word, I would have missed that life-changing experience.

It's possible to spend a lot of time reading the Word without really benefiting from it. This is not a ritual we do to please God; this is our daily feeding time, when we gain nourish-

> Keep a record as you
> read God's Word
> and it speaks to you.

ment to get us through the day. Therefore, we must read those words with an air of expectancy, looking for the truth God would speak to our hearts that day.

Keeping a Record of Your Communication With God

Some people call it "journaling," others call it a "spiritual notebook." Whatever you want to call it, I *strongly* encourage you to keep a record as you read God's Word and it speaks to you.

Again, there are as many different ways to do this as there are people, I'm sure. Some people write in their journals every day, paraphrasing what the Scripture said to them that day. My pastor recommends writing each day after reading a passage from the Bible, and answering these three questions.

1. What does this passage teach me about God?
2. Are there any promises to be believed?
3. Are there any commands to be fulfilled?

I don't necessarily write every day, but rather at those times when something in Scripture has a particularly special meaning or new understanding for me. I personally don't impose a strict rule in that regard, but I do write in it very frequently. And I write as though it were a letter to God, so it becomes not only a record but a prayer.

Why keep a record? Here are a few of the many good reasons:

- It helps you remember what God said to you through his Word.

- It helps you concentrate more as you read.

- The journal becomes a treasure house to you as it tracks your own spiritual growth.

- The journal becomes a great encouragement to you, as you remember how God spoke to you in times past.

- You'll forget many things God says to you if you don't take time to write them down.

Psalm 143:5 says, "I remember the days of long ago; I meditate on all your works and consider what your hands have done." Keeping a record—or journaling—is a great way to facilitate your memory and thereby to obey God by remembering what he has done.

I treasure my journals, which I've kept since 1983. I frequently refer to them for encouragement, for ideas to use in messages, and to remind myself of all that God has done for me in the past.

What should you use? It really doesn't matter. My good friend uses spiral notebooks. I use the cloth-covered blank books you can find at any bookstore. The only thing that is important, I think, is that it be bound in some way to keep you from losing the pages or getting them jumbled.

> Prayer is the method God has chosen to unleash his power in this world.

What should you write? Just write from your heart, in your style. Remember, no one reads this except you (unless you allow others to). You don't have to worry about your writing style, your spelling, your punctuation. No English teacher will come along to grade it! This is a book of encouragement for you. It doesn't have to be long, it doesn't have to be clever. But I believe it is most important to keep a record of what has transpired in your heart as you've read and meditated on God's Word.

Learning to Pray

Do you find it difficult to pray? Do you have trouble believing that God is really hearing you and that your prayers truly reach his ears? Have you become discouraged about praying because your prayer time seems so dry and unexciting?

Well, quite frankly, that should not surprise you, because the same enemy who doesn't want you to meditate on God's Word certainly doesn't want you to pray. Why? Because prayer is the method God has chosen to unleash his power in this world. It takes faith to pray, faith pleases God, and prayer is the channel that guides the direction of God's working among people.

Prayer is the way God changes you and me.

Prayer is not changing God's mind or trying to get God to do what we want, but it is getting hold of God's willingness to pour his power and blessing upon us.

But also, prayer is the way God changes you and me. To truly pray is to change. It makes us more Christ-like, more sensitive to God's Spirit, more loving and compassionate to others. No wonder our enemy does not want us to pray and does not want us to discover the power and joy of prayer.

In Luke 11:1 one of the disciples asked Jesus, "Lord, teach us to pray, just as John taught his disciples." If prayer was something so essential and important that Jesus prayed a lot and John taught his disciples to pray, they reasoned, and rightly so, that it would be important for them to pray and pray well. Hence the request: "Lord, teach us to pray."

Notice that Jesus didn't respond by saying, "Oh, prayer is a personal thing. It can be done in any way as long as you are sincere." No, he said, "Here's the way to pray," and he gave them a format for prayer which we have called the Lord's Prayer. In other words, by his response he said, "Learning to pray is a very worthwhile thing; you need to learn. And I will teach you." Many Christians stumble in their attempts to pray for lack of any structure or procedure. They haven't learned much about praying.

Volumes upon volumes have been written about prayer, and I am probably the least-qualified person to try to add anything meaningful to what has already been written and said. But since I've struggled with imposing this discipline in my life, I can at least share with you some suggestions for structuring your prayer life that have proven very beneficial to me.

> **Many Christians stumble in their attempts to pray for lack of any structure or procedure.**

The Master's Format for Prayer

Since Jesus is the Master Teacher, his prayer instructions are the most important ones. The model he gave us for prayer is the best. You'll find it in Matthew 6 and Luke 11. There are many excellent books on the Lord's Prayer; I recommend you read one. My favorite book on the Lord's Prayer is *A Layman Looks at the Lord's Prayer* by W. Phillip Keller.

Briefly, the Lord's Prayer teaches us that prayer should contain:

- Praise and adoration—"Our Father in heaven, hallowed be your name."
- Commitment—"Your kingdom come; your will be done on earth as in heaven."
- Petition—"Give us today our daily bread."
- Repentance and forgiveness—"Forgive us our debts, as we also have forgiven our debtors. And lead us not into temptation, but deliver us from the evil one."

The Lord gave us this prayer as a format, an outline, an example of what prayer should contain. There is nothing wrong with reciting this prayer, but that was not his purpose. He was teaching us what our prayers should contain. Therefore, when you pray, follow this simple outline. You can't go wrong; it was given to us by Jesus himself!

Pray Scripture

I've just picked up on this in the last few years, and more and more I'm praying Scripture, because then I know I'm praying in the right way for the right things. I pray Scripture in three ways:

1. *I use praise passages, which have been written down in my journal, to offer praise and thanksgiving.* It's hard to improve on the way those saints of old praised God, so I often use their words. You'll find some examples of these prayers in 1 Chronicles 17:16ff; 1 Chronicles 29:11-13; Micah 7:18; Psalm 30:11-12; Psalm 36:5-6; and Nehemiah 1:5-6. As you read the Bible, you'll find many others that you can use.

2. *As God speaks to me through his Word, I write down those verses in my journal to address any area of need in my life.* And then I pray them often. Here are some examples of ones that I have noted in my journal:

- "Lord, teach me to pray." That's a good place to start.

- "Lord, today I present my body as a living sacrifice, that it may be holy and acceptable to you, which is only reasonable. And I pray that I shall not be conformed to this world today, but shall be transformed by a renewed mind, so that I can prove your perfect will in my life today" (see Rom 12:1-2). I strongly urge you to pray this passage often. It is life changing!

- "I want to know Christ, and the power of his resurrection and the fellowship of sharing in his sufferings, becoming like him in his death" (see Phil 3:10).

- "Today, Lord, help me to think only what is true, noble, right, pure, lovely, and admirable" (see Phil 4:8). It's very important to pray about your thought life.

- "Lord, today may no unwholesome talk come out of my mouth, but only what is helpful for building others up according to their needs, that it may benefit those who listen" (see Eph 4:29). If you have as much trouble with your tongue as I do, this prayer is very important!

- "Teach me to seek the praise of God, not of people," (see Jn 5:44).

- I pray on each piece of the armor of God as outlined in Ephesians 6. In that way I'm much better prepared for "enemy attacks."

These are just a few of the Scriptures I have written in my journal, which I pray as a commitment and dedication of my life.

Now, let me tell you what happens when you start to pray Scripture like this into your life:

- Little by little progress is made in all these areas.

- You drill these passages into your mind because you pray them often. They are written down for your eyes to see frequently. Therefore, you remember them.

- Throughout the day, the Holy Spirit brings them back into your mind when you need them.

What a difference this kind of praying makes in your everyday life!

3. *Have you ever felt you didn't know how to pray effectively for other people?* Do you end up with lots of "Lord, bless So-and-so" prayers. Well, for your friends and relatives who are believers, the best thing you can do for them is pray some of the apostle Paul's prayers. Just personalize it to your friends and relatives. I'll give you one example, using *Ann* as a substitute name.

"And this is my prayer: that *Ann's* love may abound more and more in knowledge and depth of insight, so that she may be able to discern what is best and may be pure and blameless until the day of Christ, filled with the fruit of righteousness that comes through Jesus Christ—to the glory and praise of God" (see Phil 1:9-11).

Pray whether you feel like it or not. Feelings are not to be trusted.

You can't pray a better prayer for your friends and relatives than that, and there are many others as well. To list a few, Hebrews 13:20-21; 1 Thessalonians 3:12-13; 2 Thessalonians 1:11-12; Ephesians 3:16; Colossians 1:9-12 and Philemon 6.

The last suggestion I have for learning to pray is *"Pray!"* Just do it! Pray whether you feel like it or not. Feelings are not to be trusted. Usually, the feelings come once you start praying, but even if they don't, pray.

I can tell you that I never bound out of bed with warm fuzzy feelings about spending time getting to know God. It always begins with discipline. Combined with the discipline of getting up early, I have a time and place and a routine that propel me into this daily time with God. If I waited until I felt like it, it would rarely happen.

But the blessings that await you when you put this discipline in place are so great and so rich that I can't urge you enough to make this your highest priority. This is the most life-changing discipline any of us could impose. You will be amazed at the wonderful changes in you when this becomes part of your daily life. As Jesus said, eternal life is getting to know God.

Thirty-Day Challenge

Here's my challenge to you for getting to know God: Spend *one hour* at the beginning of each day for thirty days in communication with the God of all the Universe, taking advantage of your privilege as a child of God to go boldly before his throne where you can call him "Abba Father," the dearest and most intimate of terms, and where you will receive mercy and find grace to help in your time of need (Heb 4:16).

I know that seems like a lot to ask, but this is one time I want to encourage you to start BIG rather than small. This is so life changing that you just have to prove to yourself what it will do for you. I could relate many experiences from people who have accepted this challenge, and how it has brought new hope and joy and control and peace and productivity—ad infinitum—into their lives.

It is foolish economy to think that you don't have one hour a day to give to God because you're just too busy. As Bill Hybels' book title suggests, we are all *Too Busy Not to Pray*. Besides, we all do pretty much what we really want to do. If you really want to see God's power unleashed in your life, and you want to get to know God better, you can find an hour a day for time with God.

If you do this in a consistent and structured way for thirty days straight, you will be so blessed and so changed that you will wonder why you've found this discipline so difficult to implement.

Day 1: Decide what method you will use. Buy a notebook for journaling, if needed. Determine what time and place will work best for you. (Some of you may have to break your hour up into two parts.) Set your alarm early enough for one hour of quiet time with the Lord.

Days 2–30: JUST DO IT!

Make this discipline your first and highest priority. All others become much easier as you pray about them and ask God for help in this daily quiet time.

Nine

Wait Until You See What Happens!

Enjoying the Fruits of Discipline

Since you're reading this last chapter, I am hoping that means you've read most if not all of the others. And I'm praying that you have made some decisions about imposing new, needed disciplines into your life. Hopefully this book has given you some "snooze alarm gimmicks" and practical help in those areas.

Now the hard part comes. You have to do it. And as I've noted throughout the book, it is the doing that is difficult, especially at first.

After demonstrating amazing servanthood to his disciples by washing their feet, Jesus said, "I have set you an example that you should do as I have done for you" (Jn 13:15). This must have been a bit puzzling to those twelve men. After all, they were following Jesus with the idea of being part of his earthly kingdom, sitting on his right or left hand, being top guns in his

Discipline will bring great blessing into our lives.

government. And now he was telling them that they should be foot washers, taking on the lowliest of servant tasks. This did not exactly fit their image of discipleship.

Jesus went on to say, "Now that you know these things, you will be blessed if you do them" (Jn 13:17). Another puzzlement to their minds, I'm sure. How could servanthood bring blessing? They expected to be blessed with prestige, power, authority, wealth. This was their idea of their reward for serving Christ. But Jesus shattered their preconceived notions and informed them that blessing comes to them when they follow his example of servanthood. They thought that servants were there to bless other people. Jesus totally reversed that idea and said that they would be blessed by being his servant.

In the same way, discipline will bring great blessing into our lives. It seems to be a paradox that something as difficult and unappetizing as these daily disciplines could be an avenue for blessing to us. But if you will allow me to paraphrase our Lord's words, I believe that they apply very well: Now that you know how to impose needed discipline in your life, you are going to be blessed when you do it. The blessing is in the doing.

Bless Your Life

Here are some of the blessings that await you when you do what you know:

- You will like yourself so much better.

- You will shed a great deal of guilt.

- You will feel better physically and have more energy.

- You will be far more productive.

- Your relationships will improve.

- Your boss (if you have one) will be much happier with you.

- The quality of your work will improve.

- Your attitude will be much more positive.

- You'll be a much nicer person to be with.

- You'll use your time much more efficiently and effectively.

- You will greatly reduce your stress levels.

- You will look better.

- You will look younger.

- Your spiritual growth will greatly increase.

- Your life will bring far more glory to Jesus Christ.

- You'll be a much better witness to your world of your faith in Jesus.

These are not "pie-in-the-sky" promises. Take it from one who knows: These things will happen to you as you do what you know you should do.

So if only for selfish reasons, there is ample evidence that a smart person will impose needed daily disciplines. But for us who are born from above and who live for a higher purpose than our own selfish ends, we have a far more motivating reason to become more disciplined.

Martin Luther wrote in his *Theologia Germanica* about the way people deal with order and rule in their lives, which we would translate into what we mean by discipline. He said some have order only because and when it is forced on them, others do so for the rewards that will be theirs, some think they need no order and scoff at any talk about it. But then he describes how a true believer should feel about order—or discipline:

> Those who have been illumined by God and guided by the true Light.... do not practice the ordered life in expectation of reward. They do not want to acquire anything with the aid of reward, nor do they hope that they will some day reap some reward because of it. No, they do what they do in the ordered life out of love....
>
> They know, of course, that order and rectitude are better and nobler than the lack of it. So they want to keep the rules, but they also know that their salvation and happiness are not dependent on the observance of rules.

(From *Devotional Classics* ed. Richard J. Foster and James Bryan Smith [New York: Harper Collins, 1993], 148.)

None of these daily disciplines is a law
I have to keep in order to earn my salvation
or prove my worthiness to God.

How grateful I am that we are no longer under law, but grace. God's astonishing grace continues to amaze me, as I see how much grace he pours out to me. So none of these daily disciplines is a law I have to keep in order to earn my salvation or prove my worthiness to God. He and I know fully well that I am totally unworthy, and no amount of discipline could earn me his favor. His favor is given to me freely, as it is to us all.

But the very knowledge of this marvelous grace motivates me to want to please him, as I'm sure it does for you as well. Nothing cheers my heart more than to think that the Lord would be smiling down at me, pleased with what he sees in my life, knowing that I have done what was not easy for me to do simply because I love him so dearly and want so to please him.

This is the great advantage we have over those who know not our Lord Jesus Christ. We have the motivation to please Jesus, and the great reward of hearing his "Well done, good and faithful servant."

Quite frankly, I shudder at the thought of standing before Jesus someday, as we will all do, to give an account of how I've used my time, my resources, my energy, my gifts, and my abilities while here on earth as his servant, and having to face my squandered opportunities. I can somehow hear him asking me, "Mary, why did you not discipline yourself more in staying on task, so that you could accomplish more for my kingdom? There are good works left here on your list that were not accomplished because you were so disorganized or lazy or undependable." That's one scene I want to avoid.

Jesus said we will be blessed when we do what we know. If you've read this far, hopefully you know more than before. Now we're down to the doing part.

A few last reminders:

Start with baby steps. Choose the most-needed discipline that is missing in your life and set attainable goals. Don't try to do everything overnight. If you try to change too much at once, you set yourself up for failure, and that will cause you to give up. Once you reach your first goals, it encourages you to continue to higher goals.

Build discipline upon discipline. Remember that once you have some success in one area of discipline, it will be easier to implement other disciplines. Success begets success. So be encouraged that the first baby steps may seem like very slow progress, but you will build upon those small beginnings, and it will grow exponentially as you build discipline upon discipline.

When you fail, start over again. You will have days and times of failure. I believe I can say that with certainty, because if you

---

Don't let failure cause you to quit. Just start all over again!

---

don't have days of failure, you would not be reading this book! Just tell yourself, "Well, I blew it today, but tomorrow is another day and by God's grace we start afresh tomorrow."

This represents one of your potentially greatest areas of struggle. The great majority of us give up when we fail at something new. Expect failures. It will be three steps forward and two backwards at times. But that is still progress. Don't let failure cause you to quit. Just start all over again!

Pray daily about the areas where you struggle most. As a believer in Jesus Christ, you have a powerhouse of strength available to you because you have the Holy Spirit of God living in you. Turn on that power! What God has called us to do, he empowers us to do. Daily prayer will make a big difference as you face the challenges of imposing new disciplines.

You have some exciting days ahead as you begin to enjoy the fruits of a disciplined life. I would be so thrilled if you would share your stories with me and let me know what has worked for you and how your life has been blessed by implementing some of my "snooze alarm" ideas. Please let me hear from you. Here's my address:

Mary Whelchel
The Christian Working Woman
PO Box 1210
Wheaton, IL 60187
tcww@christianworkingwoman.org
www.christianworkingwoman.org

Who knows, maybe my next book will be a book of success stories. Wouldn't that be fun! Remember, the blessing is in the doing. I pray you will take what you know and turn it into action, for the glory of Jesus Christ!